# THE ADOLESCENT

# The Adolescent

## A PSYCHOLOGICAL

## SELF-PORTRAIT

## DANIEL OFFER
## ERIC OSTROV
## &
## KENNETH I. HOWARD

Basic Books, Inc., Publishers          NEW YORK

Library of Congress Cataloging in Publication Data

Offer, Daniel.
   The adolescent.

   References: p. 175
   Includes index.
   1. Adolescence. 2. Adolescent psychology. 3. Self
perception. 4. Youth—Research. I. Ostrov, Eric,
1941–     II. Howard, Kenneth Irwin, 1932–
III. Title.
HQ796.O354       305.2′3       81–66980
ISBN 0–465–00053–3 (cloth)   AACR2
ISBN 0–465–00054–1 (paper)

To our families, especially our teachers:

Raphael, Tamar, Susan, Deborah, Peter,

Lisa, David, and Rebecca

# CONTENTS

# Contents

## PART FOUR / APPENDICES

# ACKNOWLEDGMENTS

THE STUDY presented in this volume was begun in 1962, by the senior author, in the Department of Psychiatry of Michael Reese Hospital and Medical Center in Chicago, Illinois. Over the eighteen-year span of the research, the authors have received important and consistent advice from the following individuals: the late Judith Offer, Roy R. Grinker, Sr., Melvin Sabshin, William Simon, Richard C. Marohn, Joseph Adelson, and Michael F. Basch. We are grateful for their help.

This study was supported by grant HD–02571 from the Institute for Child Health and Human Development, Public Health Service; grant A70–15 from the Illinois Law Enforcement Commission; grants 4870 and 08714 from the National Institute of Mental Health, Public Health Service, and general research support grant FR–05666 from NIMH; the Institute for Juvenile Research, Department of Mental Health, State of Illinois; and the Adolescent Research Fund, in memory of Judith Offer.

The authors are grateful to the following investigators for sharing their data with us: Dr. P. Agrawal, Dr. A. G. Baikie, Dr. T. G. Brennan, Dr. M. M. Campbell, Ms. M. Carmody, Dr. R. Casper, Dr. E. Chigier, Dr. E. Coche, Dr. T. Dimperio, Ms. R. C. Egger, Mr. B. Fetrow, Dr. S. Fine, Mr. G. A. Flint, Dr. D. Fretzin, Dr. M. R. Green, Dr. H. Heath, Dr. A. S. Henderson, Dr. H. S. Hudson, Ms. H. Lander, Dr. I. L. Lewis, Dr. I. F. Litt, Dr. J. Looney, Dr. J. B. McAndrew, Dr. R. C. Marohn, Ms. J. Medak, Ms. G. Mosman, Ms. K. O'Brien, Mr. M. Offer, Dr. D. P. Orr, Dr. A.

## Acknowledgments

Petersen, Dr. M. Robin, Ms. N. R. Ross, Dr. E. Silverstein, Dr. A. Small, Ms. L. Teri, Mr. A. D. Vreeland, Dr. J. Welsch, Ms. L. Whatley, and Dr. W. H. Young.

Thanks also are due to M. Allison, J. Melton, L. Terapulsky, B. Briscoe, and M. Krause for their important contributions to the preparation of this book.

DANIEL OFFER
ERIC OSTROV
KENNETH I. HOWARD
Chicago, Illinois
January 1981

# THE ADOLESCENT

# INTRODUCTION

$\mathbf{M}$ANY SAGES in many cultures have suggested that youth is wasted on the young. And in cultures as diverse as Greece and Egypt in ancient times, to Europe in the Middle Ages, and even in our own culture today, a common theme of disapproval and despair regarding the current generation of adolescents has united adults: What have we done wrong, they ask, to deserve such terrible offspring? Adults have felt that the young lack proper respect for their elders and that they have misguided value systems. Young people have been considered unreliable, confused, moody, ascetic, or too interested in pleasure seeking—in short, persons who are incredibly self-centered. Young people have been blamed for everything from increases in crime, violence, suicide, and political upheaval to the breakdown of traditional familial and religious values.

Yet adolescents remain the torchbearers who perpetuate the sociocultural traditions of a culture from one generation to the next. In doing this, inevitably they also threaten adults, who already are disillusioned with them. By the sheer act of growing up, an adolescent sends a clear message to his parents: You are getting closer to having to face your own demise. The adolescent may also serve as a reminder of unfulfilled dreams that his elders had for themselves, dreams that now can only be fulfilled by the new, and younger, generation.

## The Adolescent

To further complicate these emotional issues, as a person proceeds from childhood through adolescence and to adulthood he wants to be his own navigator. He usually indicates to his elders that, even if the sea is stormy, he will captain his own ship.

There is probably little that either adolescents or adults can do to change how the transfer of power from one generation to another takes place, or whether it makes for relatively few or many problems. Theoreticians and clinicians, as well as patients, have tended to assume that adolescence in itself is psychologically so loaded that, even under the best of circumstances, turmoil can be expected. The immense popularity of the writings of Erik Erikson on identity attest to the universal appeal that the problems of youth hold for adults mystified by adolescents' concerns.

These issues are fraught with still more difficulties. For example, adolescents struggle with their independence at the same time that they have to learn to cope with their dramatically changing bodies and strengthened aggressive and sexual drives, and to deal for the first time as near-adults with society's social and cultural institutions. These are formidable tasks for young people. Sometimes adolescents fail to meet these challenges in an acceptable fashion. Unfortunately, many adults generalize from those adolescents who do indeed have serious psychiatric and/or social problems related to these issues to include all youngsters in this age group. The relatively untroubled adolescent is regarded as an anomaly, an unexpected pleasure. In fact, the normal adolescent has remained an enigma for most adults. And this attitude is reinforced by well-respected clinicians who state, for example, that "the upholding of a steady equilibrium during the adolescent process is in itself abnormal" (A. Freud, 1958:275); or, more recently, that "there is no other period in life as stressful in itself and as full of a variety of problems as adolescence" (Rabichow and Sklansky, 1980).

Much has been written in the past eighty years about adolescent behavior. Investigators have tried to answer a number of questions: (1) How can adolescent behavior best be understood? (2) What causes it? (3) Why do some adolescents cope well with their lives, while others have serious trouble? (4) What can we do to help those in trouble? (5) Is the normal or mentally healthy adolescent

as elusive a person as was previously thought? (6) If normal adolescents exist, what are they like?

Our own interest in the developmental psychology of normal adolescents began in 1960. At that time very little empirical work had been done involving normal adolescents. As was common then, as well as now, clinicians, counselors, and social scientists used clinical data as a basis for generalizations about normal populations. Even though normal teenagers were not studied by clinical investigators, they were assumed to have the same basic conflicts as psychiatric patients or juvenile delinquents. An excellent, though by no means unique, example is Gardner (1959), who assumed that the characteristics of the normal adolescent could be seen by observing the psychiatric patient:

> By way of illustration . . . I shall present and discuss our intake interview with a sixteen-year-old girl and the subsequent intake interview with the mother. In my opinion, these two interviews highlight most of the problems and anxieties (and defenses against anxieties) that one will meet in an *essentially normal adolescent*. (Authors' italics)

Similar use of clinical evidence can be found in Blos (1967), Josselyn (1952), A. Freud (1958), and Fountain (1961).

It has always been difficult to undertake psychological studies of normal populations. The individuals to be studied do not have the same incentives to cooperate that patients have. They obviously are not as available for investigation as are disturbed populations: One could not, under ordinary circumstances, ask a normal subject to come to a psychiatric clinic two times a week, for an hour each time, over a period of two years. Moreover, volunteers often have underlying motives—for example, the unadmitted wish to obtain psychotherapy—that make them undesirable subjects (Perlin et. al., 1958). Even with a grant to support the study of normal populations, questions will always remain about the kind of data that are collected.

In order to undertake a carefully designed study of normal adolescents it is necessary to study the complete population of a number of high schools which cover the socioeconomic spectrum that is of interest. A random number of students from a given population can be studied. Once the sample has been selected, as many students as possible (definitely over 85 percent) must be studied in order to avoid the problem of including individuals who are covertly seeking psychotherapy or help of another kind. The inquiry has to be meaningful to the subjects. To engage an uninterested individual in intensive psychotherapy creates emotional havoc and resentment. The few times such studies have been attempted, they have not worked (Eissler, 1960; Gitelson, 1954). One reason is that psychoanalysts found that when the motivation for therapy was lacking, the possibility of developing a working relationship was diminished.

In 1962, we set out to improve our understanding of the developmental path of normal adolescence by directly studying normal adolescents. Other people have described how adolescents feel about themselves, their families, and the world around them (Blos, 1961; A. Freud, 1958). Our present data are unique, however, because we have drawn from an unusually large sample of normal teenagers and we have delved into many aspects of adolescents' internal and external psychological worlds. In addition, our data span two decades and allow us to compare boys and girls from several culturally diverse countries. We also compared younger and older adolescents (both boys and girls), and teenagers living in different decades. To establish a basis for comparison, we used our methodology to study samples of deviant, physically ill, and psychologically disturbed adolescents.

Our goal here is to delve in depth into adolescents' own views of themselves. Research like this is valuable for a number of reasons. First, it is essential to have a baseline for the phenomenology of normal adolescents before anyone can appreciate the psychology of deviant adolescents. The unique contribution of our research is that it allows us to see the normal, middle-class male and female adolescent through his or her own eyes.

Second, people who work with teenagers, both troubled and normal ones, need to know what these youngsters regard as their problems. One of the jobs of teachers, parents, counselors, and mental health professionals is to be empathic with other individuals. It is important that professionals resonate with the conscious experience of people they come in contact with. Harboring false preconceptions works against that kind of communication. Having an accurate impression of what teenagers think and feel is a necessary condition for rapport and the ability to help the disturbed teenager. Our extensive investigation of adolescence allows us to offer new perspectives on this period of life to adults who work with, or live with, these young people.

Finally, a major goal of our research on adolescent self-image is to shed light on the nature of the self in general. Adolescence presents an ideal stage for better understanding the psychological aspects of the self, for it is a time of life when one can observe the changes that have occurred since childhood and the solidification that readies a young person to face adulthood. We are in a position to be able to bridge psychological theory, empirical data, and planned psychotherapeutic interventions. Our experience over the past eighteen years with the Offer Self-Image Questionnaire for Adolescents has given us the empirical base for understanding various aspects of the developmental psychology of adolescents.

# PART
# ONE

## Theory

# 1

# THE SELF:
# A THEORETICAL VIEW

WHAT IS THE SELF, and why are people interested in it in the first place? The desire to understand oneself and others may be, in part, a reflection of each person's existential aloneness, the autonomy achieved developmentally, and the awareness that each of us is a separate being. Also important is the sociocultural ethos of our highly individualistic times and society (Ostrov and Offer, 1980). For adolescents, in particular, the desire to know the self is tied up with learning how to relate to others while also acquiring a sense of separateness and autonomy, the quest to achieve what Erikson (1950) calls "identity."

One approach to understanding the self is to inquire into the origin of the word. The word "self" is defined in the Oxford English Dictionary as "that which . . . a person is really and intrinsically; . . . a permanent subject of successive and varying states of consciousness." This definition alludes to, but perhaps does not make sufficiently clear, a distinction that recurs in later psychological works, namely, a distinction between the self as observer (the subject of states of consciousness) and the self as something observed (that which a person is really and intrinsically). William James (1892) wrote that the self can be divided into two parts: (1) the self as knower, or the "I" and (2) the self as known, or the "me." This distinction arises because humans can be self-reflective; in observing another person, the observer must always take into account the fact that the other person can observe himself at the same time. Thus, to the observer, the other person often appears, to use James's terminology, as both an "I" and a "me," whereas the observed person, we can assume, experiences himself only as a "me," the person he thinks and feels himself to be; the "I," the knower, is by definition not experienced (Smith, 1978).

In a usage common to many modern theorists of the self (see Wylie, 1974; Rosenberg, 1979), the term "self" as used here will mean *only* the observed person's phenomenological experience of self, the "me." This chapter explores the philosophical and psychological underpinnings of the concept "self," a concept of crucial importance to adolescents. The book itself is a clarification of how adolescents think and feel about themselves.

The distinction between "I" and "me" emphasizes the importance of keeping in mind whose point of view about the self is being considered. We will discuss the matter in terms of an adult trying to understand the self of an adolescent. To the adult, the adolescent is a total being located in a social or historical context, among whose attributes is the way he seems to think and feel about himself. The adolescent's opinion about himself is one more fact about that "self" rather than a definitive pronouncement about its reality. The adolescent, in turn, might feel that others' opinions of him are wrong. He may ultimately feel that only his own thoughts and experiences of himself define what he really is, that only he can say what he really is. We may say that, to an adult, one way to know an adolescent is to try to understand his experiences and perceptions of his own self, what his "I" experiences and perceives his "me" to be. The adolescent, however, could believe that his self-related perceptions and experiences subsume the entire space of what constitutes the reality of himself; that what the adult tries to know as the adolescent's "me" is his entire self.

Complicating this picture is the fact that adults' opinions affect how even the most mature adolescents think and feel about themselves. By the time people reach adolescence, they can choose associates who have opinions (and selectively pay attention to only those opinions) that confirm their ongoing attitudes about themselves (Rosenberg, 1979). If the adults and the adolescents disagree, then the truth about the self becomes particularly elusive. Is the observed adolescent in the best position to know, or is there an objective truth about the self that adults are in the best position to know? Is the teenager just one more observer of his "me," whose judgment should be overridden by a consensus among seemingly objective adults, or is the observed teenager in a unique position to declare the truth about himself? Can adults infer, for example, that the adolescent really is not in touch with his anxiety? Or, conversely, is the truth about an adolescent's self-experiences and perceptions his alone to reveal or not to reveal as he chooses? It is in the answers to these questions that many insights into the nature of the self can be found.

In seeking answers to these questions, it is especially important to retain the distinction between the adolescent's and the adult's viewpoints. Knowledge of the adolescent self is very much a function of one's point of view and one's intentions. If the adult is only interested in his own point of view about the adolescent, then he may not be able to understand, and his findings may be irrelevant to, the adolescent's self. The adult may be more interested in his own assessment of the adolescent's self than in the self as the adolescent, in fact, experiences it. On the other hand, if the adult is primarily interested in the adolescent's experience as an object of knowledge for its own sake, then the adult must try to know, if it is possible, the adolescent as he experiences himself.

To illustrate these distinctions, assume that the adult is a scientist of the logical positivist school of thought. This adult might claim that the self of the adolescent is no more and no less than a construct anchored in observables that do or do not facilitate predicting and controlling the adolescent's behavior. If the observables do not enhance prediction and control, this adult might say that the self is a useless or even a chimeric concept, one more related to poetry

13

than to science. But if the self is deemed to facilitate prediction and control, the scientist might seek to measure that concept. To distinguish the self from the "person," the scientist might claim that the construct is the "me," that is, the subjective self-perceptions of the person studied; but the validity of that construct will be judged by its ability to lead to prediction and control. This scientist will only find useful a concept of self that is tied to a hypothesis that how the other thinks and feels about himself is important in predicting his behavior. If the adolescent denies the assessment of his self when this approach is taken, then his denial will be acknowledged only insofar as it correlates with a failure to predict. If the adolescent distorts, then that distortion will be meaningful only insofar as it precludes predicting or controlling his behavior.

If the adult is a psychotherapist for, or a friend or parent of, the adolescent, he might be more receptive to the idea that what the adolescent thinks and feels himself to be is important even if it is irrelevant to prediction and control or is inaccessible. If the outside observer's focus is on establishing rapport and sharing feelings with the adolescent, then his goal is facilitated by having criteria that emphasize confirmation by, and trusting in, the adolescent himself. This is because the experience of me can only be directly known to the adolescent himself, and in that sense is the adolescent's to share with or keep from others. From this perspective, the relevant way of knowing another is through empathy, a process described by Orlinsky and Howard (1975) as "tuning in" to subtle changes in the other's expressive behavior at the sensorimotor level, and by Kohut (1980) as "vicarious introspection." The goal of empathy is knowledge of the experience of another. That empathic knowing can either supplement or be an alternative to scientific predictive knowing is a theme to which we shall return.

The adolescent might agree that the scientist could know him better than he knows himself. If the scientist's inferences about his self predict the adolescent's behavior better than his own self-concepts do, the adolescent might agree that the scientist knows the adolescent's self better than he, the adolescent, does. We should not forget, though, that the adolescent may feel instead that the observer's opinion is not only wrong, but that it is wrong because the adolescent has intentionally concealed aspects of himself from the observer or has created a false opinion in the observer's mind. The adult as scientist may be more "correct" than the adolescent, even from the adolescent's point of view. The scientist also may be wrong about the adolescent precisely because the adolescent presented himself in purposeful variance from his experiences.

Each actor in the drama, in short, must live with his own doubts. The scientist must live with the possibility that he and not the adolescent is the one being predicted and controlled. The parent or friend must trust that he knows the adolescent's me because of the nature of their relationship; he must trust that he is being let into the adolescent's inner world and that a true sharing of feelings is occurring. But trust is all he has; not available to him are the pragmatic criteria of the scientist, the neutral arbiters of what can or cannot be accepted as valid scientific knowing. The adolescent, in turn, might doubt his own self-knowledge and take a scientific test to find out how he feels about himself, or he may feel that no one knows or could know his real feelings.

In knowing another, our stand must always be that of the outside observer. As such we must always rely on inferences from behavior. Smith (1950:518) wrote that "life space is not immediately given in the concreteness of experience; it is an abstract hypothetical construct, inferred by the psychologist-observer from the individual's behavior." While the adolescent's me cannot be experienced by the adult, there are many different approaches to knowing the adolescent self that outside observers may take. The choice of approach depends on why the observer wants to know the self of the other. Each adult observer will know a different truth about the adolescent; as the criteria of truth shift, so will what is considered known.

The drama between the observer and the adolescent has other implications for a definition of self. The adolescent conceptualizes himself, but he may not explicitly conceptualize every experience he has of himself. The adolescent may be motivated not to realize something about himself, either to protect self-esteem (Sullivan, 1953; Rosenberg, 1979) or to maintain a self-image that has continuity over time (Lecky, 1945; Rosenberg, 1979) or for other reasons having to do with the avoidance of anxiety (Freud, 1926). The individual also may ignore or fail to integrate aspects of himself that he considers irrelevant. In terms of the definition of the self, ignored and resisted self-conceptualizations argue for distinctions between a conscious self, a preconscious self, and an unconscious self.

The possibility of an unconscious self is particularly challenging conceptually. It suggests that an adolescent can avoid symbolizing certain experiences, that he can actively avoid drawing certain implications about himself in order to spare himself anxiety. This subject will be dealt with at greater length later, but at this point we shall note that some eighty years after Freud began writing about the unconscious, there is still a great deal of room for dispute about the exact mechanisms by which this process works and, in fact, about the very existence of the process itself.

To Kelly (1963), the self was a construct, a way of thinking about an object that happens to be one's self. The self can also be thought of as an attitude whose object is one's own self (Rosenberg, 1979). As a construct, the self can be said to have a certain range of application and a certain value when compared with other selves (Kelly, 1963). As an attitude, the self can be thought of as having characteristics such as consistency over situations and stability over time (Rosenberg, 1979). Self-dimensions such as self-esteem and self-confidence, self-esteem and ideal or desired self, and self-esteem and presented or situation-dependent self have also been differentiated (Rosenberg, 1979; Goffman, 1959).

The adolescent's self also may be usefully differentiated into discrete areas of concern. For example, the adolescent may feel differently about himself in different contexts: as a student, as a friend, as a son or daughter. To the extent that his self-feelings form broad, cohesive subgroupings, the adolescent can be thought of as having many selves or self-dimensions. In the following, some of these points will be amplified as we survey cognitive and psychoanalytic approaches to the self.

## NATURE AND DEVELOPMENT OF THE SELF

The self as the term is used here refers to the phenomenal self. It is the me as experienced or perceived by the person whom we seek to know. As theorists of the self, all the writers discussed in this section implicitly view the I as becoming self-reflective and, by definition, as developing a me, a process beginning in early childhood and reaching new heights at, but continuing beyond, adolescence. The differences among the theorists, then, pertain to their views about how the me is developed, and, just as cogently, what the nature of the me is.

### COGNITIVE APPROACHES TO THE SELF

One of the more influential theorists on the subject of the development of the self is George Herbert Mead, an American philosopher who did much of his writing in the early part of the twentieth century. According to Mead (1934), humans develop the capacity to represent themselves to themselves through the process of learning a language, and ultimately by learning to regard themselves from the point of view of other people. To explicate this process, Mead believed that a speaker must choose his words carefully in order to make communication meaningful. The speaker must assume the role of listener before speaking, in order to make certain that the listener will respond to his words in the ways he desires. In this process, insomuch as persons use verbal terms to represent reality, reality is represented by the common terminology provided by the speaker's culture. Reality is articulated in categories provided by others and, consequently, is imbued with socially accepted meanings. The perception of reality, moreover, becomes interlaced with the anticipated reactions of others.

Since one part of the listener's reality is the speaker himself, anticipating the listener's reactions heightens awareness of self as a part of objective reality. Like other parts of reality, the representation of self tends to be formed using the categories provided by the culture. Sex roles provide an excellent example. One of the

17

basic responses people learn to expect from others is that they will be assigned to a specific sex-role status. In anticipating the responses of others, persons continuously rehearse being thought of in appropriate sex-role terms. As a result, at an early age (Kohlberg, 1966) people learn to think of themselves as being intrinsically and immutably either boys or girls.

An extension of Mead's thought, one elaborated by the social interactionist school of thought (see, for example, Goffman, 1959), involves the expectation that when a person becomes aware of his ability to anticipate the reactions of others, he will act in ways calculated to maximize the probability of their reacting to him in certain ways. He learns to manipulate their definitions of the reality he himself represents. Another, more subtle, implication is that since the self is at least partly a social reality, if a person believes that others view him differently after his manipulations, he will then tend to believe the very definitions of himself that he has induced. In fact, one might reason, a change in his self-perceptions may have been one motivation for a person's having manipulated the views of others in the first place.

Piaget also discussed the cognitive development of the self. In Piaget's work, the emphasis is on the child as an active explorer and as a synthesizer of his own ways of conceptualizing reality. Awareness of self begins when the infant starts to differentiate among preverbal schema for effecting various results in the physical world. Specifically, self, body, internal world, and external world become distinguished as requiring different kinds of sensorimotor schema for the attainment of various consequences (Piaget, 1968).

Another facet of Piaget's theory involves cognitive readiness to form and differentiate concepts such as the self. Thus, implicit in the ordinary use of the word "self" is the quality of continuity over time. Correspondingly, the development of object permanence—a development achieved by the child through active experimentation with objects—is a precondition of the formation of a concept of self. Other processes, such as the imitation and internalization of the behavior of others, which greatly facilitate the formation of a self, also require a certain amount of cognitive readiness

18

prior to being initiated. The imitation of others (and events, generally) begins, in Piaget's theory, as a way of mastering and perpetuating what are preverbally experienced as external and interesting phenomena. Imitation requires the functional capacity to assimilate sounds and movements made by others into schema involving the child's own production of those events. Thus, the imitation of a wink involves the complex association of visual and kinesthetic cues and the child's reproduction of them. With differentiation from others, object permanence, and a growing ability to imitate, the self is perceived as more similar to, but still separate from, others.

According to Piaget, language consolidates developments such as these by providing words that permit distinctions between self and not-self. Representations of aspects of reality can be clearly and separately labeled ("I," "you," "me," "it"). Language shapes development by means of the social categories implicit in the words ("boy," "girl"). With time, the child becomes increasingly able to take on the role of others, a process facilitated by exposure to differences of opinion, the need to communicate with strangers, and experience with the contradictory wills of others. Concomitant with this increasing ability to take the point of view of other people is the process of decentering, which involves decreasing egocentrism and increasing objectivity about the self. With adolescence comes the development of the abilities to induce rules and to manipulate the laws of logic; at this time, the child can strive for self-consistency and also try out new ideas about himself. He can entertain the possibility of rejecting the view of others about himself. The possible connection between this trying out of new selves and the rejection of old ways of thinking, and feelings of loneliness in adolescence, has been commented upon by Kohlberg and Gilligan (1971) and Ostrov and Offer (1980).

Piaget's insights about the development of self supplement those of Mead, although Piaget emphasizes the child's own actions, explorations, and constructions of reality—his is an emphasis on the I rather than on me. Mead, on the other hand, stressed the social construction of reality, an influence Piaget would not have denied.

# Theory

Psychoanalytic writers describe the self in terms that contrast markedly with those used by Mead and Piaget. Freud, who was primarily interested in building a scientific model of the workings of the mind, wrote almost nothing about the self, probably because the self focuses on the point of view of the subject and not the observer. Contemporary psychoanalysts, however, such as Grinker (1957), Jacobson (1964), and Kohut (1971) have tried to write about a concept of the self within the traditional psychoanalytic framework. To psychoanalysts, the self is basically an organization of feelings, some of which the individual is motivated not to recognize consciously. As a result, while the self is partly conscious, aspects of the self can be split off, that is, they can exist outside of one's consciousness, and still remain influential in determining behavior or feelings.

Grinker (1957) believed the self is a system that fuses a complex array of identifications in interaction with both social and self-recognition. He stressed feelings about the self and others that are grounded in one's early interpersonal experiences. According to Grinker (1957), a child develops aspects of self at a very young age, partly through imitation, incorporation, confusion between what is inside and outside his own body, and internalization. Imitation is the same process as that described by Piaget. Incorporation is a process of becoming like a missed person. It is a way to master separation from nurturing figures through becoming like them in some ways. Confusion between what is within or outside one's own body can only occur before the self and others are clearly distinguished; one aspect of this process involves ascribing to the self feelings and sensations more correctly directed at other people. Internalization refers to children's incorporating into their own sense of their selves the affective attitudes of others toward them.

As a result of these processes, a sense of self develops that is affectually charged, and that may be largely unconscious, or preconscious (where unconscious refers to self-referent feelings and perceptions that are actively disavowed or resisted and preconscious refers to self-referent feelings and perceptions that are neither fully articulated nor actively disavowed or resisted). It is this largely unconscious, or preconscious, self that is recognized by others in social interaction and that ideally leads to the social recognition of the subject as the person he or she is. This is called "role complementarity." Social recognition, in turn, leads to self-recognition in socially meaningful terms.

Jacobson (1964) used the term "self" to mean (citing Hartmann, 1950:19) "the unconscious, preconscious, and conscious endopsychic representations of the bodily and mental self in the system ego." Like Grinker—and true to the psychoanalytic tradition—in discussing self-representations, Jacobson emphasized the emotional experiences of self, the "direct" awareness of inner experiences and not what she called indirect self-perception and introspection. Self-representations are developed in a stream that includes wishful images of the self, aggressive and sexual energy directed inward or outward, and the maintenance of self-esteem from within or without. The self, or self-representation in this language, is not so much realized or achieved as it is created by the ebb and flow of psychic energies, defense mechanisms, and interpersonal experiences, all of which occur largely at the affective level.

For Kohut (1971), the primary aspect of the development of self involves self-esteem regulation. Grandiose feelings about the self, for example, or the idealizations of parenting figures characteristic of very young children may persist into adolescence or even adulthood if not grasped by the "reality ego." Kohut's theory is replete with references to struggles to maintain self-esteem, breakthroughs of grandiose feelings, and idealizing transferences. According to this way of looking at feelings and impulses, adults and adolescents may be depressed yet grandiose underneath it all, or may be demure and, without seeing the inconsistency, overly self-admiring at the same time.

One important implication of psychoanalytic theories is that a person's self, even if it is phenomenologically defined, may include feelings and tendencies that the person is unconscious of. This implication has a parallel in the theories of Carl Rogers (1951), who maintained that perceptions about the self that would be threatening if symbolized may be denied or perceived in a distorted way. Because symbolization is avoided, important feelings and motives may not be integrated into an ongoing concept of self. Labeling a feeling may dramatically change the way it is expressed (Schachter and Singer, 1962). At adolescence in particular, the consolidation of a clearly articulated self-image may leave certain feelings unintegrated or unincorporated into the overall self-image.

The "self-system," described in Harry Stack Sullivan's theory (1953), is also instructive. Sullivan believed that the child forms a self-system that promotes security insofar as it exists in conformity with the perceived wishes of parenting figures. Sullivan wrote (1953:247) that the self-system is "the vast organization of experience which is concerned with protecting our self-esteem." A basic personality dynamic is the avoidance of anxiety by means of the maintenance of self-esteem. Self-esteem, in turn, is served by preservation of the self-system, even if the price is "selective inattention," which is the failure to recognize the "actual import of a good many things we see, hear, think, do and say" (Sullivan, 1953:374) because recognition would expand and change the self-system. What Sullivan called the "not-me" provides a dramatic example of this process of selective inattention. According to Sullivan (1953:163), the "not-me" is a "rudimentary personification" of experiences "which, when observed, have led to intense forbidding gestures on the part of the mother, and induced intense anxiety in the infant . . . [the experiences] persist in life as relatively primitive, unelaborated parataxic symbols." Sullivan (1953:316) adds that "only under exceptional circumstances are there any reflections in consciousness—that is, in awareness—of that part of one's life experience which I have called not-me—a sort of third rudimentary personification." The extreme result of this tendency to fail to incorporate certain aspects of experience into the self-system is manifested in paranoid adaptations. What was maintained before in dissociation as an "intolerable aspect of one's own personal possibilities" becomes "definitely personified as not-me—that is, as others" (Sullivan, 1953:361).

The idea that a person may have unconscious self-feelings should be distinguished from the possibility of being unaware that one has certain personality traits. The latter may refer to a person's characteristic behavioral, motivational, cognitive, or affective tendencies, tendencies that the person himself may have no phenomenal awareness of whatsoever. These tendencies are often grouped into a concept called "ego." For example, a person may be what a psychologist or some other outside observer would call "suspicious" and yet have no awareness at all that he could fairly be so designated. If his unawareness stemmed only from his never having thought of himself that way and from no one's ever having brought the matter to his attention that trait could characterize his ego but not his self. Theoretically, a failure to integrate, or resistance toward integrating, into an ongoing self-perception the perception of one's self as suspicious would be another matter.

## INTEGRATION OF COGNITIVE AND PSYCHODYNAMIC APPROACHES TO THE SELF

The theories of the psychoanalysts and of Mead and Piaget might appear to be in conflict. To Mead, the self was part of the social construction of reality that the I comes to accept; similarly, to Piaget, the self was one of many schema the child constructs in the process of making sense out of his world. But in the view of Grinker, Jacobson, Kohut, and Sullivan, the self is not just that which is consciously apprehended, but also includes feelings and wishes that are unconscious, some of which the person is motivated not to integrate into an ongoing concept of self.

Our own view is that these theories are not irreconcilable. Piaget (1973:34) wrote that while "the self is conscious of the contents of its thought, it knows nothing of the structural and functional reasons which force it to think in this or that manner." Later in the same essay, Piaget (1973:40) wrote that "awareness consists of a reconstruction on an upper level of what is already organized in another manner on a lower level." For Piaget, then, consciousness implies focusing upon and labeling with words, which hitherto may have functioned automatically and therefore unconsciously. If a person is motivated not to admit certain affective tendencies or wishes into consciousness, it may be because different consequences follow for that person from not explicitly labeling those tendencies or wishes than might follow if he did explicitly label them. The same would be true for the assimilation or nonassimilation of those tendencies or wishes into an articulated, ongoing self-concept. It is one thing, for instance, for a person to fear being rejected as a child and to know that the fear is located within himself. It is another thing for that person to become explicitly aware of the implications of those tendencies—to articulate to himself that affectively he still feels like a child. In this interpretation, the point is not repression out of conscious awareness, but rather, a motivation not to engage in the active process necessary to bring certain tendencies or wishes into fully articulated, self-conscious awareness.

What may make this process more difficult to grasp is that people would like to believe that they are fully open to self-realization. People would prefer not to believe that they are more comfortable with a dimly or fleetingly realized truth about their own selves than they are with a fully articulated, integrated self-realization. Yet the experience of psychotherapists with patients, and possibly the experience of most people with harsh truths about themselves, is that sometimes the most elementary self-realizations are vigorously resisted. Because of this, the self whose development we must account for probably should include more than a person's cognitive representations of himself to himself. The better view, in the light of all these theories, is that the self corresponds to the sum total of perceptions, thoughts, and feelings held by a person in reference to himself. These perceptions, thoughts, and feelings may be more or less clearly labeled, and may be more or less clearly articulated into an ongoing self-schema, or self-system. Yet, even if they are vigorously denied at the level of what the person tells himself (and others) about himself, these thoughts and feelings still form part of the phenomenal self, the me of the person under scrutiny.

Adolescence is a critical period with respect to the development of self. An increased ability to think logically and abstractly (Piaget, 1968) ensures a more coherent and well-articulated view of self, while richer social experience and greater knowledge ensure a more complex social construction of the adolescent's own reality. At the same time, adolescence is a stage in life rich in affective issues such as emerging sexuality, separation from family, the quest to form a new nuclear family, increased motility, and striving for vocational identity and autonomy (see, for example, Blos, 1967 and Erikson, 1950). Perhaps affective components of self emerge most clearly in this developmental stage, as self-feelings are tested in the crucible of dramatic physiological, psychological, and social changes. Or, unconscious self-feelings may be crystallized as some poignant self-perceptions or feelings split off from the conscious self-perceptions occupying the attentional field. Our position, however, is that what normal adolescents consciously know and report about themselves is much more salient than what they are motivated not to know or report. This conclusion flows from our data and our work with adolescents; it is not required by a theory of self. It is clear that adolescents, as thinking persons, can have a range of feelings that are not consciously owned or reported. Our work with adolescents, as we shall amplify later, simply does not support the view that this state of affairs is the dominant characteristic of the typical or normal adolescent.

In the discussion thus far, one issue has not yet been mentioned: the healthy self. From a scientific point of view, a self that led to inaccurate predictions on the part of the I would be a maladaptive self. In Kohut's thinking (1971), an adolescent whose conscious self walls off important self-feelings is psychologically unhealthy in that he may find himself reacting in ways he cannot explain, sometimes to the point of self-destructiveness. To Rogers and his followers, low self-acceptance, that is, a large gap between ideal self and perceived actual self, is the root of psychological disturbance. Sullivan thought walling off feelings and attitudes from the self-system was the heart of psychopathology. These theorists agree that it is good and healthy to perceive oneself accurately and to regard oneself highly.

An adolescent unable to acknowledge important self-feelings, unable to make accurate predictions about himself interpersonally, or unable to regard himself highly, could be seen as emotionally unhealthy. Assessment of the accuracy of perceptions of self-feelings or interpersonal reactions might require psychoanalytic or social psychological investigation. But low self-esteem is more easily measured. To learn about one aspect of the me—the felt, symbolized experience of the adolescent self—one question we addressed to adolescents was, in effect, "Just how good do you feel about yourself?" That their self-appraisal was accurate is a theme that recurs throughout this book.

## AN APPROACH TO THE STUDY OF THE SELF

According to Kaplan (1964), scientific knowing cannot be evaluated apart from its purpose. If the purpose is to classify and make phenomena conceptually more comprehensible, then the methodology used must be evaluated on those grounds. If the purpose is to predict and control phenomena, then the methodology used must be assessed in that light.

Scientists often try to understand phenomena by describing laws governing changes in these phenomena over time and across circumstances. The purpose of science may be said to be the construction of a "map" that describes relationships between sets of phenomena over time. Concepts delimit a band or range of phenomena that can be described clearly in just that way. The self of an adolescent can be thought of in these terms. Predictions can be made about the "shy" adolescent, for instance, or the "depressed, lonely" one. In each case the concept delimits a set of observations that enhance prediction and control. Alternatively, one might try to understand the self of an adolescent for its own sake—as a way to reach out to the I of an adolescent, to transcend the separateness that surrounds each of us. A third possibility is to reach an understanding of the self of the adolescent in an effort to enhance the adolescent's own ability to predict and control his behavior and better conceptualize his experiences.

In both scientific-predictive and non-predictive knowing of the self, empathy may be used to appreciate the subjectivity of the adolescent. In non-predictive knowing, the stress is on good communication and a good relationship between observer and observed. When predictive, causal understanding is sought, on the other hand, the locus of truth shifts from openness on the part of, and confirmation by, the adolescent to validation using a hypothetical-deductive causal model from the adult's point of view. When the adolescent's own ability to predict and control is the focus, the criteria for knowing shift to enhancement or non-enhancement of his ability to predict and control. All these approaches are viable for research on adolescence, and each can aid in trying to understand the adolescent self. The focus of this book is on the use of empathy as a way to facilitate attaining any or all of these purposes.

By definition, empathy involves the acquisition of knowing about the private meaning of behavior. As Frank (1978:312) wrote, in using empathy, "[p]resumably, information from latent nonverbal cues and preexisting preconscious images and fantasies is synthesized and emerges into awareness in the form of a visual image or conscious fantasy, which is in turn associated with an emotional experience." Schafer (1979) explained the working of empathy as involving, in part, regression in the service of the ego, including relaxation of defense and openness to archaic experience.

Empathy can also involve a more purely cognitive component (Frank, 1978 and Schafer, 1979), namely the assimilation of emotional insights into theoretical frameworks of understanding. This assimilation is reminiscent of the working of Piaget's schema and Kelly's constructs and theories. In effect, the empathic person may give the emotions he intuits an intellectual cast, responding not "innocently," to use Schafer's (1979:11–12) word, but employing instead "models of the expressive person and context, and of expressiveness itself."

Empathy requires openness to one's own experiences and openness to the experience of the other person. It also may involve the assumption of an analytic, hypothesis-building and -testing stance. Frank (1978) has shown that the prediction of behavior is theoretically and empirically distinguishable from picking up on subjective cues, and that skill in one area may not correlate with, and, in fact, may impede, skill in the other. Similarly, Frank (1978) found that training in one area may not facilitate the development of skill in the other. The implication may be that the use of empathy involves supplementary but analytically distinct uses of receptive-intuitive and hypothetico-deductive approaches to other persons.

The knowledge gained from empathy may be scientific only in the sense that it is subject to disconfirmation (Popper, 1959). The adult can ask the adolescent if his conclusions are correct and be willing to modify them if they are not. The grounds for disconfirmation are not necessarily based on causal hypotheses derived solely from the adult's point of view since the alliance is between two I's. The I of the adolescent may not be felt to be more determined causally than the adult's own self is felt to be in everyday experience. True empathic knowing looks to knowledge in the here and now, and may make no prediction other than the noncausal prediction that the adolescent will confirm that what the adult says he perceives is in fact the case. Alternatively, the adolescent's use of the knowledge gained may be a crucial component of its validity.

As an illustration of the process of knowing someone, consider the way that knowledge is gained in the parent-adolescent relationship. In seeking to know his child, a parent participates in an alliance with the I of the adolescent. The alliance between adolescent and parent allows empathy to work because it leads the child to allow the parent in, as it were, both through sharing experiences and through confirming or disconfirming the parent's inferences. A more subtle point is that in nonthreatening, supportive conditions, the child will be more able to focus upon and put into words unarticulated thoughts and feelings than would be possible in a less caring milieu. The parent also may feel comfortable in trusting that the child is not trying to manipulate his beliefs in order to prevent true understanding. To the parent, truth about the adolescent may very much involve what that adolescent feels himself to be. Furthermore, the parent's quest to know the adolescent need not involve any attempt to predict or control him. On the contrary, the parent may be most interested in facilitating the choice-making power of the adolescent, a power that by definition need not facilitate the parent's ability to predict and control.

A disciplinarian or administrator, on the other hand, may be interested only in predicting what the adolescent will do next. This adult may use empathy but only to learn "where the adolescent is at," the better to manipulate him. The irony, though, is that the very purpose of this adult may preclude the adolescent's sharing his subjective experiences to the extent necessary to make successful prediction and control possible.

The choice of theory of self, the access to data, and the result of adducing various propositions all will depend on the purposes of the adult and on the nature of the relationship between adult and adolescent. The process of understanding the self of an adolescent entails an interweaving of scientific and empathic postures, an alliance of I's in trying to understand the me of one of them. Our position is that using the scientific and the empathic approaches are supplementary and equally viable ways to study the self.

If knowledge about the self is relative, it is nonetheless attainable, providing we are clear about the perspective from which we operate. We can advantageously apply the scientific model to humans, and in terms of our interest, to adolescents in particular, without claiming a monopoly of all truth about human functioning. Similarly, we can try to appreciate others as observing, choice-making I's without blinding ourselves to the ways in which they are being driven by, or at least influenced by, forces emanating from their biographies, their physiological make-up, and their circumstances. People often use non-predictive empathic and predictive scientific points of view when relating to one another. Empathy informs scientific constructs by shaping their focus and construction, while science facilitates the process of empathic understanding with its insistence on clarifying terms and bases of understanding. In this book both approaches are used: The adolescent is seen as a perceiver and experiencer of his own self, and his me is viewed as a construct in a scientific, hypothetico-deductive system that facilitates an understanding of adolescence in general.

# 2

# THE OFFER
# SELF-IMAGE
# QUESTIONNAIRE
# FOR ADOLESCENTS

IN 1962, the Offer Self-Image Questionnaire (OSIQ) was developed as a means of tapping the feelings and attitudes that teenagers have about themselves. Since then, thousands of adolescents in this country and other countries have taken this questionnaire and shared their knowledge about themselves with us and other researchers. In this chapter, we shall describe how the OSIQ data were accumulated over an eighteen-year period; we shall also discuss the various groups studied and the exact procedures followed in the analysis of OSIQ responses. Technical details about the methodological characteristics of the OSIQ are given in Appendix A.

## THE INSTRUMENT

The Offer Self-Image Questionnaire was originally developed to provide an objective procedure for selecting a representative group of modal or normal adolescents from a larger group of high school students (Offer and Sabshin, 1963; Offer, 1969). Since that time, its primary use has been to provide a standardized and reliable means of gathering information about the phenomenal self of teenagers. The test also can be seen as an occasion for adolescents to share thoughts and feelings about themeslves with researchers. The OSIQ has become a widely used research tool; it has been administered to over 15,000 teenagers. The populations include males and females, selected from normal, physically ill, delinquent, and disturbed populations. It has been administered in rural, urban, and suburban areas in the United States, as well as in Australia, Israel, and Ireland. The samples cover the middle class; only a limited number of upper- or lower-class subjects have been tested.

The operational approach of the OSIQ rests on two assumptions. First, it evaluates functioning in multiple areas, since the teenager can master one aspect of his world while failing to adjust in another. Second, the psychological sensitivity of the adolescent is sufficiently acute to provide valid self-description. Empirical work with the questionnaire has supported these assumptions.

The OSIQ contains 130 items that cover many areas of adolescent functioning (see Appendix A). Items call for a numerical response ranging from one to six, where one corresponds to "describes me very well" and six corresponds to "does not describe me at all." To guard against response bias (in this case, the tendency to answer all items in the same direction), some items are worded positively, and others, negatively. The test scales contain unique sets of items; scale length ranges from nine to nineteen items (see Appendix A). When items are added to form the eleven separate scale scores and a total score, negatively worded items are reversed. (As explained in Appendix A, the total score is formed by averaging only ten of the eleven scale scores.) In this book and more recent articles (for example, Offer, Ostrov, and Howard, 1981A), these raw scale scores are not used. (Unlike the scores used in this book, in raw scale scores, the ones usually cited in our earlier papers, the higher a score was, the poorer the reported adjustment in the corresponding area of functioning.) Instead, use is made of standard scores that have been adjusted so that fifty equals the standard reference group mean, fifteen equals its standard deviation. In addition, standard scores are adjusted so that higher scores imply better adjustment.

## PROCEDURES

Aside from technical considerations of reliability and validity, in Chapter 1, we suggested that the self can also be investigated from an empathic perspective. As a source of data for empathic interpretation, the OSIQ works in the following way. First, subjects taking the OSIQ were simply told that we wanted to know how they think and feel about themselves. They were assured that any truthful answers were acceptable. Also, items are couched in nonthreatening terms, and since answers can be qualified as being not at all true or very true, they are more likely to reflect what subjects are willing to share rather than what they are trying to conceal. The anonymous conditions under which the test is usually given also tends to facilitate honest disclosure since it removes any obvious external reason for faking. Given a good alliance, an opportunity to communicate, and a motive to communicate accurately, one can trust that a sharing of subjective "I" experiences—empathy—has taken place.

Because they are typically seeking to establish their own identities and, thus, are intensely interested in themselves, adolescents as a group are particularly willing to share inner experiences and perceptions. Then, too, adolescents are characteristically idealistic, a quality that makes them unwilling to describe a subject of such importance to themselves falsely. Most convincing are the data, which, as we shall see, show strongly that the portraits obtained through the use of the OSIQ tended to be realistic views of adolescents' conscious inner experiences.

Not surprisingly, then, one basic strategy was to approach OSIQ data as a source of empathic knowing about teenagers' self-perceptions. We also used the OSIQ data as a means of testing various hypotheses about intergroup differences in adolescent self-image. To enhance the interpretability of the data, certain rules were used to reduce the incidence of phenomenologically invalid protocols. These rules, which resulted in the deletion of a certain number of clearly invalid protocols, are presented in Appendix A.

Once the OSIQ data were screened, frequency counts of responses were made, with responses being grouped as reflecting "endorsement" (responses 1, 2, or 3) or "non-endorsement" (responses 4, 5, or 6). The data were also scored with respect to the various scales and the total score. The following sections will describe the subjects from whom OSIQ data were gathered and the procedures followed to obtain the results that form the core of this book.

## SUBJECTS

The subjects who provided the OSIQ data can be divided into four categories: 1970s normals, 1960s normals, adolescents from other cultures, and deviant adolescents. The latter category includes subjects who were delinquent, psychiatrically disturbed, or physically ill when tested.

### 1970S NORMALS

The subjects in this category were drawn from ten United States high schools in the late 1970s and in 1980. Five of the schools were in the Chicago suburbs; two others were Roman Catholic parochial high schools in Chicago. Students in these high schools were primarily from working-class and middle-class backgrounds. One school was a public high school in rural Minnesota; another was a public school in Burlington, Vermont, with a rural and an urban population. The tenth school was a private academy in Ver-

**Theory**

mont composed primarily of upper-class youngsters. Appendix A shows a breakdown of the subjects by these characteristics. In the table, the Minnesota and Vermont public schools are identified as rural; the Chicago parochial schools, as urban; the Chicago suburban schools, as suburban; and the private academy, as upper class.

TABLE 2–1

*Numbers of Rural, Suburban, Urban Parochial School and Private Academy Students Comprising the Normal 1970s Adolescent Samples*

|  | Rural | Suburban | Urban Parochial | Private Academy |
|---|---|---|---|---|
| Young Male (Total N = 212) | 69 (33%) | 82 (39%) | 33 (16%) | 28 (13%) |
| Young Female (Total N = 373) | 82 (22%) | 223 (60%) | 25 (7%) | 43 (12%) |
| Older Male (Total N = 276) | 100 (36%) | 124 (45%) | 25 (9%) | 27 (10%) |
| Older Female (Total N = 524) | 157 (30%) | 288 (55%) | 34 (6%) | 45 (9%) |

In each school that provided adolescents for testing, the subjects were recruited with a minimum of selection bias. Study halls, classrooms, and homerooms containing a cross-section of students were used to obtain access to students. Permission was always sought and granted through the Board of Education or the school administration. We had no problems in this area. In practice, never less than 75 percent and sometimes close to 100 percent of the students asked to fill out the OSIQ actually did so. Thus, it seems fair to conclude that the sample is representative of broad masses of rural, urban, and suburban youth.

Although it would have been ideal to test students from a variety of ethnic and socioeconomic backgrounds, many schools have policies that do not allow the testing of students for research purposes. There are hints in our data that such distinctions are not very meaningful anyway. For example, Ostrov, Offer, and Howard (1980) found a great deal of overlap among middle-class, suburban, and rural youths and inner-city, lower-class youngsters with respect to values and concerns. Similarly, there was no significant effect of race or social class on self-image scales scores in the data. The limited OSIQ data collected from inner-city schools with large minority populations show no significant scale score differences when compared to data provided by the late 1970s normals. Nevertheless, the conservative conclusion is that these results can be fairly generalized only to middle-class adolescents.

Other qualifications could be made. By testing only students, we did not have the opportunity to study adolescents who had dropped out of school, a fact that further limits the generalizability of our results. Ironically, this bias would have been greater had we extensively tested inner-city schools, since the drop-out rate is much higher in the inner city than elsewhere in the country. As it is, the sampling bias is probably greater with respect to older adolescents than it is with respect to younger adolescents, because larger numbers of older adolescents have left school. Results comparing older and younger adolescents should be assessed in that light.

In essence, these qualifications describe the phrase "normal 70s subject." When we say normal we refer to the attitudes and self-conceptions of a random group of adolescents, not necessarily to psychological health (Offer and Sabshin, 1974). And when we speak of the modal or normal adolescent of the late 1970s we mean primarily lower middle-class to upper middle-class urban, suburban, and rural youths.

1960S NORMALS

Subjects in this category were tested in the early 1960s at three different suburban public high schools in the Chicago area. As a result, the 1960s normal group is somewhat more suburban and middle-class than is the 1970s normal group. Like the 1970s group, the schools from which subjects were drawn were chosen largely because they cooperated with research efforts. The 1960s subjects tested at each school constituted a respresentative sample of the student body.

# Theory

## ADOLESCENTS FROM OTHER CULTURES

When this book was written, we had usable data from three countries other than the United States: Australia, Israel, and Ireland. The Australian data were collected in the early 1960s from private and public schools. Adolescents in a large youth organization and from several kibbutzim in the middle and late 1970s provided us with our Israeli data. The Irish samples were drawn from public and private schools in Dublin and its environs in the middle and late 1970s. In Appendix D, for the reader's interest, an Irish emotionally disturbed sample is presented as well. Readers interested in a detailed exposition comparing Irish disturbed and normal samples are referred to Brennan and O'Loideain (1980).

## DEVIANT ADOLESCENTS

The emotionally disturbed group represents a pooling of many samples drawn during the 1970s from psychiatric facilities throughout the United States and Canada. Samples include an inpatient facility in the Midwest, an outpatient clinic in British Columbia, and a residential treatment center in Texas. The disturbed group is diagnostically and demographically heterogeneous. The subjects have in common only the fact that all were emotionally disturbed enough to warrant psychiatric treatment.

Similarly diverse are the delinquent subjects. Many were residents in state hospital inpatient units for disturbed juvenile delinquents. Others were in residential treatment programs affiliated with diversionary programs for adolescents. The states involved included Illinois, Texas, Virginia, Arizona, and California. Like the disturbed adolescents, therefore, the delinquent adolescents had only one thing in common: All had been identified as being in conflict with the law.

The diseases suffered by the physically ill youngsters included severe acne, marked pubertal delay, hypertension, kidney disease, and cystic fribrosis. Some adolescents in the physically ill group, however, were only referred for suspected physical problems. The subjects were drawn from facilities in St. Louis, Chicago, Atlanta, and various cities in California; all data were collected in the late 1970s. As was true of the other deviant groups, the only thing they had in common was that each youth was identified as having, or potentially having, a serious physical problem.

## ANALYSES

### THE MODAL ADOLESCENTS OF THE LATE 1970S

The first task was to determine what the modal adolescent thinks and feels about himself or herself. To achieve this goal, the late 1970s normals were divided into four groups: younger male, younger female, older male, older female. A response was identified as characteristic of late 1970s normal adolescents when that response was either endorsed or negated by 80 percent or more of youths in all four groups. Endorsement was defined as responding with either a one (describes me very well), a two (describes me well), or a three (describes me fairly well). A four (does not quite describe me), five (does not describe me), or six (does not describe me at all) constituted a negation. This rating system revealed a picture of the modal, late 1970s adolescent with respect to each of the various dimensions of the self in our study.

### AGE AND SEX COMPARISONS AMONG LATE 1970S NORMAL ADOLESCENTS

Having depicted the self-image of the modal adolescent, we shifted our attention to self-image differences between male and female and younger and older adolescents. Statistical tests were performed using age and sex as independent variables and the various scale scores as dependent variables. These statistical tests allowed us to determine whether the various scale scores were significantly affected by age, sex, or a combination of the two.

To explicate any significant sex or age effects, we moved to the item level. Consistent item endorsement differences of 5 percent or more were considered to illustrate significant age or sex effects on particular scales. Thus, if the analyses of variance with respect to a certain scale showed a significant sex effect, a male–female percent endorsement difference of five points or more for an item on that scale for both age groups would be interpreted. To be interpreted, the item percentage differences would have to be in the same direction as the scale score difference. A significant interaction effect of age and sex on a particular scale would be exemplified by a reversal of five points or more. The only other rule was that an item that showed a percent endorsement difference of ten points or more would be interpreted. These items would be retained without regard to the significance of the corresponding scale score test results.

## GENERATION, CULTURE, DEVIANCE, AND THE SELF

To explicate contrasts in self-image according to generational, cultural, and psychosocial designation, each group's scale scores were reduced to a set of standard scores. As an artifict of the standard scoring procedure, each scale score mean for the 1970s normals equals fifty, while the standard deviation is fifteen. For the other groups, scale score means were derived by counterbalancing each group by age and sex and pooling the remaining subjects' standard scores. For example, in the 1960s normals data, the smallest age-by-sex cell was the older males (N = 128). To counterbalance this group, 128 subjects were chosen at random from each of the remaining three cells. The standard scores of all the subjects chosen were then averaged for each scale. Thus, 1960s normals standard score scale averages were derived for N = (approximately) 512 subjects (4 × 128). We did not simply take averages of averages across the four cells for any one group because doing so would not have permitted the calculation of appropriate standard deviations. The same procedure was followed for delinquent, disturbed, physically ill, and Irish and Israeli groups.

In practice, the groups were not compared to one another. Instead, the 1970s normals were compared to each of the other groups, and disturbed and delinquent subjects were compared. Appendix D shows the data that allow for comparisons of any other two groups.

To explain significant scale score differences, those items showing consistent percentage endorsement differences across all four age-by-sex cells were identified. As before, to be retained for interpretation, the differences had to be in the same direction as the difference in scale score means. For example, suppose that the 1960s normals were significantly higher than the 1970s normals on Scale 1. In that case, items would be selected on Scale 1 that showed more positive percent endorsements for 1960s versus 1970s young males, and for 1960s versus 1970s young females, and so forth.

## THE FIVE SELVES

When the OSIQ was developed, items were clustered into eleven separate scales, each representing a dimension or aspect of the self. Time and experience has taught us that the scales can be more meaningfully clustered into five dimensions: the psychological, social, sexual, familial, and coping selves. These different selves were made up as follows:

The Psychological Self
    Scale 1:  Impulse Control
    Scale 2:  Emotional Tone
    Scale 3:  Body and Self-Image
The Social Self
    Scale 4:  Social Relationships
    Scale 5:  Morals
    Scale 9:  Vocational and Educational Goals
The Sexual Self
    Scale 6:  Sexual Attitudes
The Familial Self
    Scale 7:  Family Relationships
The Coping Self
    Scale 8:  Mastery of the External World
    Scale 10:  Psychopathology
    Scale 11:  Superior Adjustment

The results described in the following chapters were obtained from testing these various aspects of the perceived self of adolescents.

PART

# TWO

## Results

# INTRODUCTION

T HE RESULTS SECTION includes five chapters titled "The Psychological Self," "The Social Self," "The Sexual Self," "The Familial Self," and "The Coping Self." The five chapters cover the 130 items that comprise the eleven scales of the OSIQ. Each group of scales describes a specific part of the total self.

One part of each chapter is devoted to the common themes that unify the four normal groups of adolescents: younger (13–15 years old); older (16–18 years old); boys, and girls. Where significant differences exist between age groups and sexes, they are described.

The basic data presented in the beginning of each chapter describes adolescents in the late 1970s. Because the self-system of adolescents may change from generation to generation, and because it also may be strongly influenced by the culture in which the adolescents have grown up, the next section in each chapter presents a cross-time and cross-cultural perspective of the self-image of normal adolescents. To what extent does time and the social changes it brings about affect the self-image of normal adolescents? What kind of impact does the social environment have on adolescents? Or, to be more specific, can cross-cultural differences be diciphered with this questionnaire?

The next section in each of the five chapters compares and con-

## Results

trasts the normal adolescents with the adolescents who suffer from physical illness, and with adolescents who are psychiatrically disturbed or socially deviant. Of particular interest are the ways that psychiatric and social problems affect the self-system of the adolescent. To be known to one's peers, family, school friends, and to the community at large as a disturbed adolescent must affect how people view the young person. This, in turn, affects the feelings the teenager has about himself or herself. Because the deviant adolescents differ cognitively and affectively from normal teenagers, they must have a different view of their selves. The differences should tell us more about the problems deviant adolescents believe they have. It should also help to clarify the nature of the self-image of normal adolescents.

# 3

# THE PSYCHOLOGICAL
# SELF

**M**UCH has been written about the psychological sensitivity of the adolescent. Adolescence is a period when one leaves the protected harbor of childhood and enters the open sea of adulthood. It is an age of increasing sophistication and cognitive complexity. There are several ways to understand the internal world of the adolescent. It can be inferred from his behavior in a social field. We can also tap the adolescent himself, who can provide a direct line to his own concerns, feelings, wishes, and fantasies. Taking this latter approach, we assessed the psychological self of the adolescent using the three scales that deal with the emotions the teenager experiences, his sense of control over his impulses, and his conception of his body. These scales constitute the occasion for teenagers sharing information with us about their psychological selves. The scales discussed in the chapter are (1) Impulse Control, (2) Emotional Tone, and (3) Body and Self-Image.

# Results

## THE PSYCHOLOGICAL SELF OF THE NORMAL ADOLESCENT

The OSIQ results, shown in Table 3–1, indicate that normal young people in our culture enjoy life and are happy with themselves most of the time. The vast majority of adolescents studied stated that they are happy, strong, and self-confident. The adolescents do not feel inferior to others, including their peers, and they do not feel that others treat them adversely.

TABLE 3–1

*The Psychological Self of the Normal Adolescent: Percent Endorsement for Items Affirmed or Denied by 80 Percent or More of Each Normal Sample*

| Item No. | Item | Boys | | Girls | |
|---|---|---|---|---|---|
| | | 13–15 yrs. | 16–18 yrs. | 13–15 yrs. | 16–18 yrs. |
| 44. | I feel relaxed under normal circumstances. | 93 | 90 | 88 | 93 |
| 68. | I enjoy life. | 91 | 90 | 87 | 92 |
| 123. | Usually I control myself. | 87 | 87 | 94 | 92 |
| 99. | I feel strong and healthy. | 89 | 86 | 85 | 85 |
| 32. | Most of the time I am happy. | 83 | 85 | 85 | 88 |
| 100. | Even when I am sad I can enjoy a good joke. | 86 | 80 | 83 | 82 |
| 23. | I feel inferior to most people I know. | 19 | 17 | 16 | 14 |
| 94. | When others look at me they must think I am poorly developed. | 20 | 15 | 20. | 13 |

The normal adolescent also reports himself to be relaxed under usual circumstances. He believes that he can control himself in ordinary life situations, and he has confidence that when presented with novel situations, he will find himself prepared. Normal adolescents generally believe that they have control over their lives.

Approximately 50 percent of the teenagers stated that they were anxious (See Appendix B, Table B–2). Because most adolescents also say that they do not feel tense most of the time, the anxiety described appears to pertain only to new and unusual situations. It is even possible that the teenagers were describing their feelings while taking the psychological test itself. At any rate, anxiety is one feature of the otherwise generally strong, positive psychological self-image most teenagers claimed.

In another area, that of body image, the data indicate that normal adolescents feel proud of their physical development, and that the vast majority of them believe that they are strong and healthy. This is not surprising since a feeling of physical health usually goes hand in hand with positive psychological feelings.

SEX, AGE, AND THE PSYCHOLOGICAL SELF

The effects of sex and age on the psychological self were assessed using a two-way analysis of variance. Only sex differences were significant. There were no age or interaction effects of sex and age. The sex effects were concentrated in the Emotional Tone and Body and Self-Image scales. Scores on these scales showed that, in general, adolescent girls have significantly more negative feelings about their bodies and their emotional states than do adolescent boys. Table 3–2 shows the seven, out of twenty-eight, items that exemplify the significant sex differences measured on the Emotional Tone and Body and Self-Image scales. The adolescent boys present a much more positive feeling than do girls about their bodies and physical development. Some other items indicate that the girls feel ashamed of their bodies more frequently, feel ugly and unattractive, and feel less good about recent changes in their bodies than do the boys. An analogous effect also occurs with respect to certain affective items. Adolescent girls describe themselves as being sadder, lonelier, and more vulnerable than boys. They are more sensitive to their internal world than the boys are. These findings are true for younger and older adolescents girls. In the area of self-control, girls state more often than do boys that they at times have fits of crying that they cannot control.

# Results

TABLE 3–2

*Sex Differences in the Psychological Self of the Normal Adolescent: Percent Endorsement for Items Differentiating Boys from Girls*

| Item No. | Item | Young (13–15) | | Old (16–18) | |
|---|---|---|---|---|---|
| | | Boys | Girls | Boys | Girls |
| 17. | At times I have fits of crying and/or laughing that I seem unable to control. | 31 | 47 | 26 | 47 |
| 66. | I feel so very lonely. | 16 | 24 | 15 | 22 |
| 130. | I frequently feel sad. | 26 | 31 | 20 | 29 |
| 38. | My feelings are easily hurt. | 40 | 58 | 37 | 66 |
| 6. | The recent changes in my body have given me some satisfaction. | 76 | 61 | 75 | 62 |
| 57. | I am proud of my body. | 77 | 57 | 80 | 51 |
| 90. | I frequently feel ugly and unattractive. | 26 | 46 | 21 | 42 |

There were no significant age differences in any of the three scales. Of thirteen items that showed a consistent age difference for boys and girls, however, twelve items favored the older teenagers. As a trend, therefore, older adolescents state that they have fewer problems than do younger ones.

## GENERATIONAL CHANGE, CULTURE, AND THE PSYCHOLOGICAL SELF

Adolescents in the 1960s had a more positive psychological self than adolescents in the 1970s. Despite this disparity, however, a great deal of uniformity exists across the generations. Adolescents in the 1960s had higher scale scores on all the three scales related to the psychological self. In standard score terms, the mean for the Impulse Control scale was 58, for Emotional Tone the mean was 54, and for Body Image it was 56 (see Appendix D). As stated in Chapter 2, the mean for each scale for the 1970s normals was

50, with a standard deviation of 15. Each of the 1960s group's scores was significantly different from the corresponding scores of the 1970s adolescents.

In order to further our understanding of these differences, we examined the endorsement frequencies of both groups item by item. Items were selected for interpretation when there was a consistent difference in endorsement across the age/sex subgroups between the 1960s and the 1970s groups. For eight items, teenagers in the 1960s responded in a more positive way. None of the twenty-eight items showed more positive results for the 1970s in contrast to a decade earlier. According to differences at the item level, adolescents in the 1960s appeared to master better their inner feelings and impulses than did their 1970s counterparts. Teenagers in the 1960s had less fear of being overwhelmed. They also saw themselves as being less volatile than did 1970s teenagers. Similarly, adolescents of the 1970s were more sensitive, feared being easily hurt, and were more worried about their health than were 1960s teenagers. The 1970s generation of adolescents were not as secure about their body images as their peers of a decade earlier were. They also reported having more overt problems and believed that they were more emotional than did 1960s adolescents.

In contrast to the marked difference in adolescents' self-images across time, very little difference emerged in the cross-cultural analysis (see Appendix D). The self-images of American teenagers were very similar to those of adolescents from Australia, Israel, and Ireland.

## Deviance and the Psychological Self

Physically ill adolescents (see Chapter 2 for descriptions of the illnesses) had worse emotional tone and body image than did their normal peers (see Appendix D). The physically ill adolescents were, as might be expected, more concerned about their health. They thought that their bodies were less attractive than those of normal adolescents. The normal adolescents saw themselves as consistently happier than did the physically ill adolescents. The normal teenager's ability to cope with emotional stress was broader, and this group felt more relaxed than did the physically ill adolescents. In addition, physically ill adolescents reported feeling inferior to their peers.

Between normal adolescents and delinquents, there was a significant difference in the Emotional Tone scale. The other two scales, although not significant, show that the juvenile delinquents had lower self-images in the Impulse Control and Body and Self-Image scales. It is of interest to note, however, that the juvenile delinquents did not view themselves as having problems with the control of aggression. They did not believe that they were violent. They did, however, see themselves as sad, anxious, lonely, and very unhappy. They believed that they got less out of life, both in terms of the present and when viewing their futures. Many juvenile delinquents continuously worry about their health and think of themselves as being physically vulnerable.

The psychiatrically disturbed adolescents described themselves as having good control of their impulses. As did the juvenile delinquents, they believed that they do not get violent. Other scale scores indicate that disturbed adolescents have more problems with mood and body image than do normal adolescents. More than delinquent adolescents, disturbed adolescents saw themselves as depressed, withdrawn, anxious, and very unhappy. They worried about their bodies and health, and they believed they were poorly developed. Their images of themselves in the future did not satisfy them, and they could not bring themselves to enjoy life.

When comparing the juvenile delinquents to the psychiatrically disturbed adolescents, the former tended to have a more suspicious, even paranoid flavored, posture toward others. The delinquents were more hostile and angry than were the disturbed adolescents, yet they claimed to be happier and to enjoy life more than did the psychiatrically disturbed. The delinquents attested to having good feelings about their bodies more often than did disturbed adolescents.

To summarize, the most salient findings in this chapter were that normal adolescents had positive psychological self-images and that males had better self-images than the females did. No cross-cultural differences emerged. Physically ill adolescents had a disturbed body image and felt badly about themselves. The juvenile delinquents' psychological selves were decidedly poorer than those described by normal adolescents, but by far, the poorest psychological selves were the ones described by psychiatrically disturbed adolescents.

# 4

# THE SOCIAL SELF

IN THIS CHAPTER, adolescents' perceptions of their interpersonal relationships, their moral attitudes, and their vocational and educational goals are considered. Three OSIQ scales reflect these areas of self-perception; these are Social Relationships, Morals, and Vocational and Educational Goals. Of particular interest is the adolescent's view of his or her social field as it is exemplified in these three scales. Adolescents are often described in terms of the friends they have, the company they keep, and the values they hold. Some social scientists have claimed that adolescents have their own subculture, with its own values and standards. Therefore, we were particularly interested in finding out whether teenagers subscribed to adult middle-class morality and vocational ideals. In the three scales, each covering a part of the social field, we looked carefully to see whether the adolescents' views corresponded to those of the larger social system.

TABLE 4-1

*The Social Self of the Normal Adolescent: Percent Endorsement for Items Affirmed or Denied by 80 Percent or More of Each Normal Sample*

| Item No. | Item | Boys | | Girls | |
|---|---|---|---|---|---|
| | | 13–15 yrs. | 16–18 yrs. | 13–15 yrs. | 16–18 yrs. |
| 70. | A job well done gives me pleasure. | 94 | 95 | 97 | 98 |
| 83. | I like to help a friend whenever I can. | 93 | 92 | 96 | 99 |
| 58. | At times I think about what kind of work I will do in the future. | 92 | 92 | 93 | 95 |
| 88. | Being together with other people gives me a good feeling. | 92 | 90 | 95 | 95 |
| 79. | I feel that there is plenty that I can learn from others. | 90 | 93 | 92 | 95 |
| 37. | I am sure that I will be proud about my future profession. | 88 | 85 | 86 | 84 |
| 124. | I enjoy most parties I go to. | 85 | 84 | 86 | 85 |
| 20. | Only stupid people work. | 5 | 5 | 3 | 2 |
| 14. | I feel that working is too much responsibility for me. | 7 | 6 | 7 | 6 |
| 48. | Telling the truth means nothing to me. | 11 | 12 | 3 | 3 |
| 67. | I do not care how my actions affect others as long as I gain something. | 14 | 15 | 10 | 7 |
| 63. | I would rather be supported for the rest of my life than work. | 16 | 16 | 8 | 11 |
| 62. | I find it extremely hard to make friends. | 17 | 15 | 13 | 13 |

## The Social Self of the Normal Adolescent

The highest endorsed item, "A job well done gives me pleasure," shows the work ethic in its purest form. Judging by the adolescents' responses, in American culture, it is a universal value. Both boys and girls are unreservedly work oriented. They say they will be proud of their future professions, and that they will like their work. They seem to believe there will be a job waiting for them, ready to be taken when they are ready to take it. The notion of a career is part of their everyday world. Similarly, they also state that they do not wish to be supported by someone else; their ethics clearly tell them that they are better off working than being supported for the rest of their lives.

Normal adolescents enjoy the company of others, and good feelings result from having group social experiences. They can learn a lot from others, they say, and they like to help their friends. They regard social relations as a process of give and take, and they report being able to exchange feelings with others. They state that they value social relationships from both the pragmatic and hedonistic points of view, and they do not have any difficulties making friends. That they do not consciously exploit others is evident from Table 4-1, Item 67. They deny that they do not care how their actions affect others. On the other hand, more than half also denied that "an eye for an eye and a tooth for a tooth does not apply to our society" (See Appendix B, Item 116.) This finding tempers the benign image the adolescents have presented so far. It suggests that a majority of the adolescents believed that if they were hurt, they would lash back without necessarily attempting to understand the circumstances that provoked that hurt.

As a group, these adolescents see themselves as making friends easily. They believe that they will be as likely to be successful socially and vocationally in the future as they are now.

SEX, AGE, AND THE SOCIAL SELF

The Social Relationships scale showed no sex differences while the Morals and Vocational and Educational scales did show significant sex effects. At the same time, there were no age or interaction effects of sex and age. The Morals scale showed that adolescent girls had significantly higher moral attitudes as well as more positive attitudes toward their future vocations. The girls' work values and ethical values were higher than those of the boys. Consistent sex differences on eight of the twenty-nine Social Self items exemplify these significant sex effects.

Adolescent girls also affirmed social values much more strongly than did adolescent boys. For example, the girls were more concerned with other people and would not hurt anyone "just for the heck of it" (Table 4–2, Item 5). Girls denied more strongly than did

TABLE 4–2

*Sex Differences in the Social Self of the Normal Adolescent:*
*Percent Endorsement for Items Differentiating Boys from Girls*

| Item No. | Item | Young (13–15) | | Old (16–18) | |
|---|---|---|---|---|---|
| | | Boys | Girls | Boys | Girls |
| 86. | If others disapprove of me I get terribly upset. | 34 | 44 | 34 | 44 |
| 5. | I would not hurt someone just for the "heck of it." | 78 | 87 | 79 | 89 |
| 30. | I would not stop at anything if I felt I was done wrong. | 39 | 24 | 37 | 20 |
| 40. | I blame others even when I know that I am at fault. | 43 | 25 | 34 | 25 |
| 48. | Telling the truth means nothing to me. | 11 | 3 | 12 | 3 |
| 46. | I would rather sit around and loaf than work. | 27 | 17 | 23 | 16 |
| 63. | I would rather be supported for the rest of my life than work. | 16 | 8 | 16 | 11 |
| 104. | At times I feel like a leader and feel that other kids can learn something from me. | 75 | 63 | 78 | 69 |

# Results

boys that telling the truth meant nothing to them. Although most normal adolescents would rather work, surprisingly, girls affirmed this value even more strongly than did boys. Boys appeared to be more autonomous and less other-directed than were girls. For example, boys affirmed more strongly that they would not stop at anything if they were "done wrong." The boys also did not agree as much as the girls with the statement "If others disapprove of me I get terribly upset." In the same vein, the boys also more often said they felt more like leaders than did the girls.

There were no significant age differences in any of the three scales. Of thirteen items that showed a consistent age difference for boys and girls, however, all favored the older teenagers. As a trend, therefore, older adolescents of both sexes report a more positive social self-image.

GENERATIONAL CHANGE, CULTURE, AND THE SOCIAL SELF

On the whole, the adolescents' social self was more consistent across the generations than it was disparate. The differences that we did find are significant and noteworthy, but they represent only part of the total picture. As was true for the psychological self (see Chapter 3), a large minority—eight out of twenty-nine items—indicated strong differences between the 1960s and the 1970s adolescents. In all eight instances, the teenagers of the 1960s had more positive self-images. At the same time, in the majority of the items, twenty-one, there were no consistent differences between the generations.

All three scales showed that teenagers had more positive social self-images during the early 1960s than their counterparts did in the 1970s. Of particular interest is the Morals scale; the 1960s subjects had the highest standard score—fifty-nine—of any of the eight basic groups studied. This indicates that the 1960s adolescents had somewhat more stable and well-structured ethical standards than other groups. In the 1970s, young people have turned more inward and have a greater concern for themselves and less for their social environment.

The 1970s teenagers do not feel socially inept by comparison to the 1960s adolescents. They feel comfortable in their own small groups, and they feel good when they are with their friends. Adolescents in the 1970s, however, seem to feel less secure than did teenagers of the 1960s in the larger school or community environment and in making friends. The adolescents from a generation ago more often stated that they confided in others than did 1960s adolescents. Today, teenagers say that if you confide in others, you might open yourself to being hurt. The teenagers of the late 1970s and 1980 also appear to feel somewhat more vulnerable than did their peers of a generation ago. They also more often state that they are sensitive. The 1970s adolescents object to being corrected even if they believe that they can learn from the criticism. The 1970s adolescents get more upset if others disapprove of them than the 1960s teenagers did. They also prefer being alone more often than their peers of the 1960s. It seems that the 1970s generation is only really comfortable with peers whom they know very well; in other social situations, they report often feeling out of place.

The work ethic was just as strong in the 1960s as it was in the 1970s. Adolescents in both decades get pleasure from work well done; this was one of the highest endorsed items in the whole questionnaire. Adolescents believe that school and studying is a very important part of their life, and they often think about what kind of work they will do in the future.

In the cross-culture analyses, Australian, Israeli, and Irish adolescents were compared with American teenagers on the three scales comprising the social self. In general terms, when American youths were compared with those from the other countries, Americans reported more positive social self-images.

# Results

## Deviance and the Social Self

No significant differences between the social self of physically ill adolescents and normal adolescents were observed. Inspection of the items, however, revealed some small differences. In morals and work ethics, the two groups are very similar. Both normal and physically ill adolescents reported having pride in their future professions, thinking about their vocations, and getting pleasure from work and learning from others. One of the few items that did show a difference indicated that physically ill teenagers believed that working was too much of a responsibility for them. It is possible that the physically ill adolescent is making a correct observation about himself. Yet, on other items physically ill adolescents state that they are optimistic about their future but at the present time feel somewhat overwhelmed by everything that has happened to them. The physically ill adolescents also state that they had a harder time making friends, were sensitive to being rejected, and often felt out of place at parties and picnics. All together, on four items out of twenty-nine concerning the social self, the physically ill adolescents described themselves as being poorer adjusted than did normal adolescents. Never did the normal adolescents describe themselves as being more poorly adjusted than the physically ill adolescents.

In comparing the juvenile delinquents with the normals on the social self-image, we find statistically significant differences in the Morals and Vocational and Educational Goals scales. There was a trend for differences to occur in the Social Relationships scale. Juvenile delinquents described themselves as being different from normal adolescents on eighteen out of the twenty-nine items constituting these three scales. The delinquent adolescents do not see themselves as sociable beings; they do not see themselves as being friendly to other people. They are solitary individuals: One out of every three prefers being alone to being with others. Among the normals, only one out of every five adolescents prefers being alone to the company of others.

The Morals scale shows that delinquents do not tend to deny their lack of ethics. A significant minority state that telling the truth means nothing to them; they also say that they like to associate with teenagers who "hit below the belt." The work ethic is still prevalent among juvenile delinquents, but not to the extent that it is among normal teenagers. Thus, delinquents are more likely to say that work is too much responsibility and that only stupid people work. Moreover, delinquents were less certain that they would be proud of their future profession. With regard to the Morals scale, the disturbed adolescents strongly disapprove of the hit-below-the-belt item. They also disapprove of revenge. On the other items in this scale, the differences between normal and disturbed teenagers are minimal.

On the Social Relationships and the Vocational and Educational Goals scales, the disturbed adolescents showed notable differences from the normal teenagers on ten out of nineteen items. The results suggest that the disturbed adolescents have difficulties in their relationships with friends. They are not as interested in same sex or opposite-sex friends, and they do not get as good a feeling from being with others as do normal teenagers. The disturbed adolescents have some difficulties in making friends, and at times, they feel out of place at parties. They doubt their ability to work and to feel proud of their work in the future. Disturbed adolescents project a sense of vulnerability and insecurity.

When the social self of delinquents is compared to that of disturbed adolescents, in seven out of twenty-nine items there were consistent differences. The disturbed adolescents stated that they felt more vulnerable to the feelings of others and they also felt that they could learn more from others then the delinquents did. The major differences between the two groups appeared in the Morals scale. In five out of ten items, the delinquents held a moral position that was notably different from that held by disturbed adolescents. In comparison with disturbed adolescents, delinquents more frequently endorsed the value of revenge and violence for the sake of violence. They also were more likely to profess a disregard for the truth and for the effects of their actions on others.

To summarize, the normal 1960s adolescents had a more positive social self-image than did those a decade later. The 1960s teenagers had a particularly high moral attitude. Older adolescents, in general, report more positive social self-images than do younger ones. Female

# Results

adolescents had higher morals scores than males. All teenagers highly endorsed work values. The physically ill adolescents showed awareness of their very real limitations. The delinquents had a low score and, in contrast, the disturbed adolescents had a high score on the Morals scale. The disturbed adolescent group was more negative about their social selves than were the other groups.

# 5

# THE SEXUAL SELF

THE INTEGRATION of emerging biological drives into the psychosocial life of the teenager can be described as the quintessence of adolescence. It is on the success or failure of this process that so much of the young person's future life depends. The development of sexuality is important to the adolescent, his family, his peers, and his culture.

The adolescent is keenly aware of the development of the sexual urge. How he copes with his sexual feelings and impulses during adolescence serves as a template for his future sexual behavior. The adolescent adapts to his sexuality in a way quite different from the way he copes with his other inner feelings. In fact, sexuality for adolescents is a separate dimension that is not correlated with the others (Offer, Ostrov, and Howard, 1977); because of this, it is treated separately here. With respect to this vital area, our strategy was straightforward: We simply asked adolescent boys and girls how they felt about their sexual experiences and behavior. The Sexual Attitudes scale was used to obtain our findings.

## Results

### THE SEXUAL SELF OF THE NORMAL ADOLESCENT

In general, the findings show that normal adolescents are not afraid of their sexuality. Seven out of ten adolescents stated that they liked the recent changes in their body. Both boys and girls strongly rejected the statement that their bodies were poorly developed, and both boys and girls indicated that they had a relatively smooth transition to emerging sexuality. Nine out of ten subjects said no to the statement: "The opposite sex finds me a bore." A majority of the subjects stated that having a friend of the opposite sex was important to them.

#### SEX, AGE, AND THE SEXUAL SELF

Adolescent boys appear to be more open to their sexuality than are the girls. They think about sex more often, say that dirty jokes are fun at times, and deny that it is hard for a teenager to know how to handle sex in a right way. Adolescent boys also more often report that they attend sexy shows.

Among the boys, there are no general age differences with regard

TABLE 5–1

*Sex Differences in the Sexual Self of the Normal Adolescent: Percent Endorsement for Items Differentiating Boys from Girls*

| Item No. | Item | Young (13–15) | | Old (16–18) | |
|---|---|---|---|---|---|
| | | Boys | Girls | Boys | Girls |
| 16. | It is very hard for a teenager to know how to handle sex in a right way. | 24 | 34 | 22 | 28 |
| 28. | Dirty jokes are fun at times. | 84 | 73 | 82 | 73 |
| 77. | I think that girls (boys) find me attractive. | 64 | 55 | 73 | 65 |
| 80. | I do not attend sexy shows. | 38 | 57 | 41 | 58 |
| 117. | Sexual experiences give me pleasure. | 86 | 60 | 87 | 76 |
| 122. | I often think about sex. | 80 | 54 | 77 | 60 |

to their sexual self-images. Some strong age differences occur among adolescent girls (see Table 5–1). The most dramatic instance concerning age differences is illustrated by the following item: "Sexual experiences give me pleasure." Older boys did not endorse this item more than did younger boys, but older girls affirmed this item much more frequently than did younger girls. Similarly, while there were no comparable developmental differences among boys, older girls were more likely to think about sex than were younger adolescent girls. The one age difference that did hold for both sexes was only a trend for older teenagers to show more confidence about their physical appearances than did younger teenagers.

GENERATIONAL CHANGE, CULTURE, AND THE SEXUAL SELF

There were no significant differences among adolescents' responses across the four cultures on the Sexual Attitudes scale. Neither were there any significant differences between the 1960s and 1970s teenagers. In both generations, two out of three teenagers state that they often think about sex. In other words, they are aware of emerging sexual feelings, and are willing to acknowledge them. In both decades, three out of four teenagers state that it is not difficult for teenagers to handle sex in the right way. Nine out of ten teenagers are not frightened by thinking or talking about sex.

In two out of ten items on the Sexual Attitudes scale, strong differences existed between the generations. The 1970s adolescents more often stated they enjoyed openly "dirty jokes" than did 1960s teenagers. Adolescents from the 1970s also more often stated that they felt that sexually they were way behind. Whereas in the 1960s less than one out of ten teenagers reported being "sexually way behind," by the 1970s more than one out of five felt this way.

## DEVIANCE AND THE SEXUAL SELF

The Sexual Attitudes scale shows significant differences between the physically ill and the normal adolescents. The physically ill adoles-

## Results

cents saw themselves as having poorer sexual self-images than did their normal peers. The physically ill stated that they did not think often about sex. They were aware that "sexually [they are] way behind," but they said this did not bother them much. They also said that having a friend of the opposite sex was not important. Similarly, their responses indicated that they do not see themselves as being physically attractive. The physically ill adolescent is aware of his problems in this area, and his sexual attitudes appear to be shaped accordingly.

The juvenile delinquents had only a slightly higher score on the Sexual Attitudes scale than did the normal adolescents, mostly because they believe more often than do normal teenagers that they are attractive to persons of the opposite sex. In contrast, delinquents reported thinking less often about sex, and they did not believe that sex was particularly important.

The disturbed adolescent has a slightly lower score on the Sexual Attitudes scale. Like the delinquent, he, too, thinks about sex less often than the normal teenager. However, disturbed adolescents are less confident about their physical attractiveness than are delinquents.

In summary, the majority of adolescents are not afraid of sex and find their sexuality pleasurable. Males are more open to sexual feelings than are females. The data do not indicate that any meaningful shifts in attitudes toward sexuality took place between the 1960s and the 1970s, and there were no differences cross-culturally. The one American group that had considerably lower sexual self-images than did the others were the physically ill adolescents. The disturbed adolescents as well as the juvenile delinquents did not significantly differ in their sexual self-images when compared to normal teenagers, but differences in attitude toward their own physical attractiveness did emerge.

# 6

# THE FAMILIAL SELF

THE FEELINGS AND ATTITUDES teenagers have toward their families are crucial for the overall psychological health of adolescents. It seems reasonable to assume that a child who grows up in a family that is stable, open about its feelings, and able to change as the needs of its members change will have a reasonable chance of growing up relatively unscathed emotionally. The poorly functioning or broken family has been blamed for many of the problems that confront the psychiatrically disturbed or delinquent adolescent. The family system provides the first line of defense for the growing child in the social world. If that system malfunctions, it is more likely than not that it will have a negative impact on its members. A well-functioning family unit does much to ensure that its members will grow up mentally healthy. If everything else is kept constant, the family will contribute relatively more to the positive development of adolescents than any other psychosocial variable.

# Results

## THE FAMILIAL SELF OF THE NORMAL ADOLESCENT

The normal adolescents we studied do not perceive any major problems between themselves and their parents. They believe that their parents are proud of them, and they feel close to their parents. The adolescents do not present any evidence of a major intergenerational conflict. The generation gap so often written about is not in evidence among the majority of subjects we studied (see Table 6–1). They perceive their parents as being satisfied with them, and they do not seem to harbor bad feelings toward their parents. Moreover, these feelings seem to extend through time. Not only do these teenagers have positive feelings toward their parents in the present, but they feel that these good feelings have been true in the past. In addition, they expect that these positive feelings will persist into the future.

TABLE 6–1

*The Familial Self of the Normal Adolescent:*
*Percent Endorsement for Items Affirmed or Denied*
*by 80 Percent or More of Each Normal Sample*

| Item No. | Item | Boys | | Girls | |
|---|---|---|---|---|---|
| | | 13–15 yrs. | 16–18 yrs. | 13–15 yrs. | 16–18 yrs. |
| 112. | Most of the time my parents are satisfied with me. | 87 | 86 | 89 | 85 |
| 15. | My parents will be disappointed in me in the future. | 6 | 6 | 6 | 8 |
| 95. | My parents are ashamed of me. | 8 | 7 | 5 | 7 |
| 106. | I have been carrying a grudge against my parents for years. | 8 | 11 | 11 | 11 |
| 118. | Very often I feel that my mother is no good. | 11 | 12 | 12 | 10 |
| 21. | Very often I feel that my father is no good. | 16 | 17 | 18 | 16 |

The results also indicate a feeling of mutual satisfaction between parents and teenagers. The parents are viewed as being patient and optimistic toward their adolescent children. They are seen as people who can be counted upon. The adolescents also viewed their parents as sharing good relationships with each other. Seven out of ten adolescents believe that they have a say in family decisions. That the adolescents do have minds of their own is indicated by the fact that a significant minority maintains that they are right even when their parents are strict. This also illustrates that normal adolescents do maintain a sense of autonomy within the harmonious family.

The most impressive findings on familial self-images are that eighteen out of nineteen items strongly indicate that the adolescents have positive feelings toward their families. At least seven out of ten normal adolescents indicate that they experience good feelings toward their parents and toward their own role in their families. The majority of the adolescents believe that they will be a source of pride to their parents in the future. They think their parents are reasonable and patient with them, and they state that they feel they understand their parents.

SEX, AGE, AND THE FAMILIAL SELF

In contrast to the other areas of self-image, we found no significant differences in age and/or sex with regard to the familial self. This illustrates, again, the consistency of positive feelings toward the family that exist among normal teenagers.

GENERATIONAL CHANGE, CULTURE, AND THE FAMILIAL SELF

No significant cross-cultural differences existed, although there was a tendency on the part of teenagers in the other three cultures to describe their relationships with their families in even more positive ways. There were significant differences between the 1960s and the 1970s adolescents in the familial self-images. Before we describe these differences, however, it should be stressed that the striking finding was the similarities that existed across generations. There were no dramatic shifts in the relationships between parents and their adolescent children between the 1960s and the 1970s.

Five items out of the total of nineteen did show consistent differences between the generations. Teenagers in the 1960s described their families in less negative ways than did their peers in the 1970s. In the 1960s, the parent is described as a patient, reasonable adult who knows what he is doing. In the 1970s, the teenager is more inclined to say that although his parent may be satisfied with him, the adolescent is not necessarily so satisfied with the parent. Family members in the 1970s seemed to be somewhat more distant with each other, and there were signs of a decrease in cohesion. The parents of the 1960s and 1970s are described by the teenagers of those times as seeming satisfied with their children. On the other hand, the parents in the 1960s are seen as more patient, and the family is seen as more democratic than was the case in the 1970s.

## Deviance and the Familial Self

The juvenile delinquents and the psychiatrically disturbed adolescents showed a significantly and remarkably different view of their families than did either the physically ill or the normal adolescents. Juvenile delinquents were more negative in seventeen out of nineteen items than were normal adolescents. Psychiatrically disturbed adolescents were more negative in thirteen out of the nineteen items in the Family Relationships scale. On the other hand, the physically ill adolescents showed differences from the normals in only three out of the nineteen items. In Table 6–2, items having salient intergroup differences are shown. To highlight intergroup differences, item percentages were averaged across sex and age groups.

In broad terms, we find that the physically ill teenagers state more often than do the normals that they believe that they will be a source of pride to their parents in the future. They also state, more than normal subjects do, that they are a bother at home sometimes. What the statements seem to say is that the physically ill teenagers do not blame their families for their disabilities but they keenly feel the burden they present. Nevertheless, the impression that one gets when comparing these two groups is that they are very similar.

68

## TABLE 6–2
### Percent Endorsement of Familial Self Items for Normal and Deviant Groups
*(Percentages are averaged over sex and age.)*

| Item No. | Item | Normal | Physically Ill | Juvenile Delinquent | Psychiatrically Disturbed |
|---|---|---|---|---|---|
| 4. | I think that I will be a source of pride to my parents in the future. | 81 | 86 | 71 | 66 |
| 9. | My parents are almost always on the side of someone else, e.g., my brother or sister. | 32 | 37 | 35 | 31 |
| 15. | My parents will be disappointed in me in the future. | 7 | 12 | 16 | 15 |
| 21. | Very often I feel that my father is no good. | 17 | 22 | 25 | 24 |
| 24. | Understanding my parents is beyond me. | 19 | 25 | 34 | 26 |
| 26. | I can count on my parents most of the time. | 76 | 74 | 66 | 67 |
| 51. | Most of the time my parents get along well with each other. | 75 | 70 | 62 | 64 |
| 55. | When my parents are strict, I feel that they are right even if I get angry. | 56 | 63 | 58 | 51 |
| 60. | When I grow up and have a family, it will be in at least a few ways similar to my own. | 76 | 62 | 50 | 60 |
| 64. | I feel that I have a part in making family decisions. | 71 | 66 | 67 | 65 |
| 71. | My parents are usually patient with me. | 80 | 79 | 64 | 69 |
| 73. | Very often parents don't understand a person because they had an unhappy childhood. | 30 | 28 | 42 | 32 |
| 85. | Usually I feel that I am a bother at home. | 23 | 36 | 43 | 42 |

# Results

TABLE 6–2 *(Continued)*

| Item No. | Item | Normal | Physically Ill | Juvenile Delinquent | Psychiatrically Disturbed |
|---|---|---|---|---|---|
| 87. | I like one parent much better than the other. | 28 | 30 | 42 | 34 |
| 95. | My parents are ashamed of me. | 7 | 12 | 24 | 23 |
| 102. | I try to stay away from home most of the time. | 28 | 29 | 49 | 46 |
| 106. | I have been carrying a grudge against my parents for years. | 10 | 13 | 26 | 19 |
| 112. | Most of the time my parents are satisfied with me. | 87 | 81 | 58 | 65 |
| 118. | Very often I feel that my mother is no good. | 11 | 13 | 18 | 18 |

With respect to the psychiatrically disturbed and delinquent adolescents, the data show there are significant and striking differences in their feelings about how satisfied their parents are with them. Nine out of ten normal adolescents feel their parents are satisfied with them, compared to only six out of ten delinquent and disturbed adolescents. The latter two groups present themselves as deviating more from the familial value system as they perceive it. The disturbed and delinquent teenagers do not share their parents' standards as often as do either the physically ill or the normal teenagers. The disturbed and delinquent adolescents also believe more often that their parents are ashamed of them, and that they will not be a source of pride to their parents in the future.

The normal adolescents have good feelings toward their families. When they are grown up, 76 percent of the normal teenagers would like to have a family similar to their own. Only 60 percent of the disturbed adolescents and 50 percent of the delinquent adolescents want to emulate their families (see Table 6–2, Item 60). To the normal adolescent, the family appears to be a place where one can feel comfortable and wanted. By comparison, a much higher percentage (43 percent) of delinquent and disturbed adolescents affirm that "they usually are a bother at home." Possibly as a direct result, the disturbed and delinquent groups say that they stay away from home much more frequently than do their normal peers.

The feelings that delinquent adolescents had toward their families were compared with those of disturbed adolescents. The delinquents stated more often that they just could not understand their parents. They thought that this might be a result of their parents having had unhappy childhoods. The delinquents showed more antipathy toward their parents, were angrier, more alienated, and carried more grudges than did the disturbed adolescents. The latter showed some understanding, although it was considerably less understanding than either the physically ill or the normal adolescent showed.

In summary, the major finding in this chapter is that normal teenagers (males and females, younger and older) describe the family as a harmonious and well-functioning social system. The differences between the 1960s and the 1970s adolescents were relatively minor, and centered around the 1970s adolescents describing less satisfaction with their parents. No significant cross-cultural differences were found. The physically ill adolescents were similar to their normal peers. The one deficiency in the family system that they affirmed was directed at themselves: They felt they were a burden to their families. Disturbed and delinquent adolescents clearly had bad feelings toward their parents. Both groups stated that they did not share their parents' values as often and as completely as did the normals. They did not see themselves as being an integral part of a cohesive family structure.

# 7

# THE COPING SELF

COPING OR ADAPTATION focuses on the strength an individual possesses. An adolescent copes with his internal and/or external world by integrating all his psychological tools. He combines the energy available to him with the ego strength he has. The less he is encumbered by psychopathological signs, symptoms and syndromes—see the new edition of the *Diagnostic and Statistical Manual*, published by the American Psychiatric Association (DSM III, 1980)—the more he is able to cope with stress that comes his way. Individuals vary in their coping abilities; they adapt in different ways to seemingly similar internal states or environmental stress (see, for example, Hamburg, Coelho, and Adams, 1974). The three scales used to evaluate the coping self in this study are Mastery of the External World, Psychopathology, and Superior Adjustment. The Psychopathology scale measures the signs and psychopathological symptoms the adolescent states he has, if any. The other two scales allow the adolescent to describe how he copes with his world (see Table 7-1).

## TABLE 7–1

### The Coping Self of the Normal Adolescent:
### Percent Endorsement for Items Affirmed or Denied
### by 80 Percent or More of Each Normal Sample

| | | Boys | | Girls | |
|---|---|---|---|---|---|
| Item No. | Item | 13–15 yrs. | 16–18 yrs. | 13–15 yrs. | 16–18 yrs. |
| 105. | I feel that I am able to make decisions. | 87 | 89 | 92 | 90 |
| 19. | If I put my mind to it, I can learn almost anything. | 88 | 87 | 87 | 82 |
| 39. | When a tragedy occurs to one of my friends, I feel sad too. | 80 | 83 | 92 | 97 |
| 89. | Whenever I fail in something I try to find out what I can do in order to avoid another failure. | 87 | 84 | 89 | 87 |
| 76. | When I decide to do something I do it. | 83 | 83 | 86 | 85 |
| 109. | I feel that I have no talent whatsoever. | 7 | 9 | 12 | 13 |
| 25. | I do not like to put things in order and make sense of them. | 10 | 11 | 10 | 9 |
| 107. | I am certain that I will not be able to assume responsibilities for myself in the future. | 11 | 15 | 9 | 7 |
| 111. | When I am with people I am bothered by hearing strange noises. | 16 | 13 | 14 | 12 |
| 22. | I am confused most of the time. | 12 | 15 | 20 | 20 |

# Results

## THE COPING SELF OF THE NORMAL ADOLESCENT

Normal adolescents face life situations with little fear and with a reasonable amount of confidence. They are empathic with their peers, which leads them to be able to identify positively with others. A theme similar to the one in Chapter 4 on social relationships emerges. Normal adolescents are comfortable in their social world and adjust well to it. They are hopeful about their future, and they believe that they can actively participate in activities that will lead to their success. They seem to have the skills and confidence necessary for carrying this hope through to fruition. They are optimistic and enjoy challenges; they try to learn in advance about novel situations. They believe that they are just as able to perform as their peers are. Normal adolescents exhibit the willingness to do whatever work is necessary to achieve their goals. They like to put things in order. Moreover, even if they fail, they believe that they can learn from experience.

The normal adolescents deny the symptoms listed in the psychopathology scale. On the whole, the adolescents see themselves as being without major problems. This does not mean, however, that everybody in the normal samples said he or she did not have problems. A significant minority does not feel very secure about their coping abilities. About one out of five normal adolescents, the data indicate, feels empty emotionally and finds life an endless series of problems without solutions in sight. A similar number of adolescents state that they are confused most of the time and say they hear strange noises. In other words, although most of the subjects state that they are doers and get pleasure from putting things in order, some are uncertain about what is going on around them and what their capacity to affect the world is. Still, the decisiveness of the vast majority of our subjects comes through strongly in our data.

### SEX, AGE, AND THE COPING SELF

There was an interaction effect between sex and age on the psychopathology scale. Young adolescent girls described themselves as sicker

74

TABLE 7–2

*Sex Differences in the Coping Self of Normal Adolescents:*
*Percent Endorsement for Items Differentiating Boys from Girls*

| Item No. | Item | Young (13–15 yrs.) | | Old (16–18 yrs.) | |
|---|---|---|---|---|---|
| | | Boys | Girls | Boys | Girls |
| 22. | I am confused most of the time. | 12 | 20 | 15 | 20 |
| 36. | Sometimes I feel so ashamed of myself that I just want to hide in a corner and cry. | 18 | 38 | 15 | 33 |
| 126. | I do not have many fears which I cannot understand. | 74 | 67 | 75 | 67 |
| 127. | No one can harm me just by not liking me. | 74 | 67 | 71 | 62 |
| 39. | When a tragedy occurs to one of my friends, I feel sad too. | 80 | 92 | 83 | 97 |

than the other three groups (older girls, young adolescent boys, and older adolescent boys). No age difference showed on the Mastery and Superior Adjustment scales.

A significant sex difference points to considerably greater confusion among the girls than among the boys (see Table 7–2). Adolescent boys report fewer fears that they cannot understand, or for that matter, fewer fears that bother them. The girls more often experience feelings of shame. Adolescent girls also report that they are more empathic than adolescent boys. They report feeling more attached to their relatives and friends than do boys. In general, the girls' faith in their coping abilities is strong, but not quite as strong as that of the adolescent boys. Girls, on the other hand, are more interpersonally and affiliatively oriented than are boys according to their own self-report.

GENERATIONAL CHANGE, CULTURE, AND THE COPING SELF

In comparing adolescents across the two generations, in both time periods out of every ten subjects nine said they were action-oriented and able to make decisions. They deny the presence of serious psychopathology and present themselves as active copers and doers. The differences that exist are, therefore, subtle. Although there are statistically significant differences on all three scales across the generations, the differences between adolescents in the 1960s and the 1970s are neither basic nor dramatic. In all, sixteen out of the total of thirty-eight items in the three scales showed consistently higher endorsements in the 1960s than in the 1970s. Adolescents in the 1960s reported higher self-confidence than those of the 1970s. They averred that they met their various life challenges with more ease than did their cohorts a decade later. The teenagers in the early 1960s more often created an impression that they felt that the world was an exciting place, and they exhibited a certain amount of flair or élan that is lacking in today's teenagers. More often than their 1970s peers, the 1960s adolescents put forward a view of themselves as functioning with relative ease in the world around them.

With regard to the cross-cultural differences, for the first time, significant differences exist between the four cultures. The Israelis measured higher than the Americans on all three scales (see Appendix D). The Australians (who were tested in the 1960s and, therefore, have to be compared to the 1960s standard scores) and the Irish score more poorly than the Americans on all three scales. The findings show that the American adolescents, as expected, are more action-oriented than the other cultural groups. When they decide to do something, they usually just go ahead and do it. The Israelis are similar, but they find the world an even more exciting place than their American peers do. The Israeli youth seem to be saying that the more they have to deal with adversity, the better, and within limits, the better they become at coping. The Irish and the Australian teenagers are more predictable and more homogeneous. They do not feel as secure about their own worth as do the Americans and the Israelis. They also show more uncertainty about their talents. Both Irish and Israeli youth share a feeling that their lives are hard and more difficult more than do the Australians and the Americans. The Israelis are more trusting than the Americans, and the Americans are more trusting than either the

Irish or Australian adolescents. It is possible that the Israelis, who openly state that they feel they have realistic fears, reflect the fact that adversity can sometimes bring people closer together. More than the Americans, Israeli adolecents enjoy solving difficult problems and believe that they will be able to assume responsibility in the future. The Irish and the Australian adolescents do not enjoy solving difficult problems as much as either the American or the Israeli adolescents do. Altogether, the American and the Israeli adolescents present themselves as active copers and doers, and while the Irish and Australian adolescents can also cope, they present more doubts about their abilities, and they come across as slightly more dependent and passive than Americans and Israelis.

## DEVIANCE AND THE COPING SELF

The three deviant groups—the physically ill, the psychiatrically disturbed, and the delinquent adolescents—all scored lower than did the normal adolescents on the three coping scales (see Table D–1). The deviant group as a whole report more often than does the normal group that they give up easily and feel at times that they would "rather die than go on living." The deviant adolescents also state that they find it hard to establish friendships more often than do the normal teenagers.

When the three deviant groups are examined separately, certain specific patterns that identify them as separate diagnostic (in the broad sense of the word) groups emerge. The physically ill adolescents say they feel more socially vulnerable than do normal adolescents. They report that it is harder for them to meet new people and to make friends easily. They describe themselves as being more self-conscious and clinically depressed. In all other aspects, the physically ill teenagers are very similar to normal adolescents. Specifically, they do not believe that they have more overt psychiatric signs and symptoms than the normal adolescents do.

The juvenile delinquents and the psychiatrically disturbed differ from the normal group in several ways. Both groups more often say they find life "an endless series of problems without solutions

# Results

in sight" than do the normal adolescents. Both deviant groups more frequently state they are confused, ashamed of their behavior, and that they perform poorly academically. The deviant adolescents also say that they have difficulty in anticipating the future, a coping strategy that normal adolescents state is of considerable help to them. The psychiatrically disturbed group measures significantly lower than the delinquent group on the Mastery scale. It seems that the delinquents find the world a more exciting place in which to live; they also state more strongly than do psychiatrically disturbed youngsters that they are action-oriented, and hence, they have a good ability to cope with external reality (even if it is realistically dangerous). The delinquent more often describes himself as disturbed than does the psychiatrically disturbed adolescent. (This discrepancy is discussed on page 113.) The juvenile delinquent more often states that he repeats things just to "be sure he is right" than do any other subjects in our study. As opposed to the other groups, the delinquents describe themselves as being more continuously on the go, but more often than not, they have little sense of knowing where they are going.

In summary, the normal American teenager sees him or herself as a competent individual who is able to resolve the problems that come his way during the adolescent years, without too much pain, suffering, doubt, or indecision. The adolescents of the 1960s did not differ in any significant way from their peers in the 1970s, with the possible exception that more teenagers in the 1960s found their world an exciting one in which to live. Both normal boys and girls see themselves as being very competent, with the boys tending to describe themselves as somewhat better able to master their environments than was true among the adolescent girls. On the other hand, according to the self-report data, normal adolescent females were somewhat more empathic than their male counterparts. The coping self-image scales are the only ones in which major cross-cultural differences emerge. The Israeli adolescents describe themselves as slightly more competent than did the Americans. On the other hand, the American adolescents reported adapting better than did either the Irish or the Australian adolescents. The deviant groups, as a whole, saw themselves as coping poorly with life. The physically ill were very close to the normal, in that they denied any gross psychopathology, but they state that they have problems coping with the social world. Disturbed and delinquent adolescents cope most poorly with their world, according to the data they provided. The delinquents, in particular, presented a picture of being overwhelmed with problems that they could not solve.

# PART

# THREE

## Discussion

# 8

# A VARIETY
# OF ADOLESCENT
# EXPERIENCES

THE DATA in Chapters 3 through 7 were based on reports from thousands of adolescents from a variety of backgrounds. In this chapter, these results will be discussed in terms of their theoretical implications. Past studies of adolescents' self-images will be used as the context for an evaluation of OSIQ results.

## THE NORMAL ADOLESCENT

The most dramatic of the OSIQ findings are those that permit us to characterize the modal American teenager as feeling confident, happy, and self-satisfied—a portrait of the American adolescent that contrasts sharply with that drawn by many theorists of adolescent development, who contend that adolescence is pervaded with tur-

# Discussion

moil, dramatic mood swings, and rebellion (Hall, 1904; A. Freud, 1958; Erikson, 1950; Blos, 1967).

## THE TURMOIL THEORY OF ADOLESCENCE

The turmoil theory proposes that adolescents normally undergo significant disruption in their personality organization. This disruption, in turn, leads to psychological disequilibrium, tumult, and mood swings. The typical adolescent, this theory proposes, fluctuates in his functioning and manifests unpredictable behavior. The adolescent is viewed as needing to go through this crisis in order to separate from his parents and develop his own identity. If he does not go through turmoil during the adolescent years, he cannot, by definition, grow into a mentally healthy, mature adult.

The turmoil theory of adolescent development has held sway among experts for over a century. It can be traced to romantic writers of the late eighteenth and early nineteenth century.

In *The Sorrows of Young Werther* Goethe described adolescent Werther, the protagonist, in the following terms:

> Sorrow and discontent had taken deep root in Werther's soul and gradually imparted their character to his whole being. The harmony of his mind became completely disturbed; a perpetual excitement and mental irritation, which weakened his natural powers, produced the saddest effects upon him . . .

Werther, who in the novella shoots and kills himself, seems an unlikely example of normal adolescence, yet viewed in terms of theories such as those of G. Stanley Hall and A. Freud, Werther's functioning emerges as only a rather extreme example of an adolescence normally marked by unhappiness, discordance, and unsettling behavior. The fact that Kiell (1959), writing in this tradition, cites Werther's inner struggles as an example of the "universal experience of adolescence" serves to underscore the point.

G. Stanley Hall (1904), in a theory that no longer has many

adherents, stated that individual development recapitulates human evolutionary development. Adolescence is viewed as corresponding to the prehistoric period, when the human species began to break with the dictates of instinct, and culture became preeminent. The source of stress and instability is the radical nature of the transition that is taking place. Unfortunately, even though Hall failed to ground his theory in careful observation, his description of adolescence as a time of great turmoil has persisted, buttressed, for the most part, by theorists writing in a psychoanalytic tradition.

Anna Freud (1946:158) represents the most extreme of the psychoanalytic views. She wrote:

> The struggle between the two antagonists, the ego and the id, has scarcely ended [in latency] . . . before the terms of agreement are radically altered by the reinforcement of one of the combatants. The physiological process which marks the attainment of physical sexual maturity is accompanied by a stimulation of the instinctual process, which is carried over into the psychic sphere in the form of an influx of libido.

As a result, Anna Freud goes on to say that "aggressive impulses are intensified to the point of complete unruliness, hunger becomes voracity and the naughtiness of the latency-period turns into the criminal behavior of adolescence." In the struggle between ego and id

> there are two extremes in which the conflict may possibly end. Either the id, now grown strong, may overcome the ego, in which case . . . the entrance into adult life will be marked by a riot of uninhibited gratification of instinct. Or the ego may be victorious, in which case . . . the id-impulses of the adolescent are confined . . . and there has to be a constant expenditure on anti-cathexes, defense mechanisms, and symptoms to hold it in check.

She then cites asceticism and intellectualization as examples of defense mechanisms used by adolescents to cope with intensified instinctual demands.

In 1945, Fenichel, another psychoanalytic writer, took up the same theme in his authoritative book titled *The Psychoanalytic Theory of Neurosis*. After talking about the "biological intensification

# Discussion

of sexual impulses at puberty," Fenichel (1945:112) says, characteristically:

> Fears and guilt feelings which originally were connected with the accompanying Oedipus fantasies are now displaced to the masturbatory activity. Adolescent personalities react differently to these fears and guilt feelings; they may take sides more with the drive and try to fight the anxiety . . . or they may, more frequently, side with the anxiety and the parents, and try to fight instinctual temptations as well as rebellious tendencies. Often they do both successively or even simultaneously.

Fenichel concludes by saying: "Many neurotics give an impression of adolescence. They have not succeeded in getting on good terms with their sexuality."

More recent psychoanalytic writings put forward similar views. In 1967, Blos, a major contributor to the psychoanalytic literature on adolescence, wrote: "Adolescence is the only period in human life during which ego regression and drive regression constitute an obligatory component of normal development." Earlier, in 1962, he had written: "A profound reorganization of the emotional life takes place during early adolescence and adolescence proper, with attendant and well-recognized states of chaos."

To Blos, adolescence is characterized by "excessive motility," "overwhelming" affect, and a "keen" self-awareness. It is characterized by a turmoil that only "abates with a gradual strengthening of controlling, inhibiting, guiding, and evaluative principles which render desires, actions, thoughts, and values egosyntonic and reality-oriented." That Blos's views are not atypical of psychoanalytic thinking is shown by reference to similar statements in Deutsch (1967), Geleerd (1961), Jacobson (1961), Josselyn (1952 and 1967), Laufer (1966), Pearson (1958), and Rabichow and Sklansky (1980). As further examples of the pervasive influence of the turmoil theory of adolescence, the interested reader might also study Eissler (1958), Fountain (1961), Ackerman (1958), and Coleman (1961). Even in as recent a publication as the DSM-III (1980:66), adolescent turmoil is seen as part of normal development: "Normal conflicts associated with maturing, such as 'adolescent turmoil,' are usually not associated with severe distress and impairment in occupational or social functioning." This is particularly striking, since the authors of the DSM-III pride themselves on sticking closely to observable behavioral patterns. In this instance, they may have swayed far away from empirical observation.

## HOW TEENAGERS VIEW THEMSELVES

How do these theoretical statements compare with the data presented in this book? To us, it is clear that among our data, there is almost nothing suggestive of marked turmoil among adolescents. With respect to normals' sexual selves, the findings are particularly cogent in this regard. In psychoanalytic theory, the intensification of sexual desires at puberty plays a major role in creating adolescent turmoil, yet the majority of the teenagers we studied are proud of their bodies, not unhappy about recent changes in their bodies, and are able to cope with and find pleasure in their sexuality.

Another example where our data differ is in the area of familial attitudes of the normal adolescents we studied. These attitudes conflict with another pervasive theme in psychoanalytic and some sociological theories, which states that the generation gap between teenagers and their parents (Freud, 1913; Bettelheim, 1965; Feuer, 1965) is a prominent fact of adolescence. According to these theories, adolescents' emerging sexuality and vigor threaten their parents, who, in turn, try to reinstitute control over their children's surging impulses. The task of separation from the parents is an onerous one for both parties, generating hostility, defensive clinging, and rejection (Parsons, 1965). Judged by their self-reports, however, normal adolescents feel no such intense conflict. Instead, they say, they and their parents respect one another, share good feelings about one another, and have mutual confidence in the continuation of good relationships.

## TURMOIL THEORY AND OUR FINDINGS

There are several explanations for the clear discrepancy between our results and those predicted by the turmoil theory. One explanation is quite straightforward. The turmoil theory is simply wrong

## Discussion

in that it is not applicable to the vast majority of adolescents. Turmoil theory, from this perspective, may accurately describe the feelings and attitudes of some adolescents, but these adolescents are a special subgroup.

Another possibility, one that the turmoil theorists would apply, is that our results are the product of subject distortion. Under this rubric exists the possibility that our normal subjects deliberately distorted the truth when they described themselves as happy, able to cope, and at peace with their families. Perhaps to appear in a good light, perhaps to maintain their privacy, one could contend, our subjects did not reveal the true magnitude of their negative feelings. An analogous explanation is that the normal teenagers we tested unconsciously distorted the truth (see Chapter 1 for a discussion of the unconscious self).

The problem with the distortion hypotheses is that they do not explain our data. If our subjects were consistently trying to show themselves in a good light, they failed in some puzzling instances. Why, for instance, did 53 percent of our normal subjects say that they are anxious? Theoretically, among negative affects, anxiety would seem among the most likely to be subject to defensive denial. The ability of the normal adolescents to acknowledge their sexuality and aggression argues to the same effect. According to Anna Freud (1946), Blos (1962), and many other authors cited earlier, teenagers typically handle aggressive and sexual urges by defensively denying them, by turning to intellectualism and asceticism. Yet the adolescents studied here showed no such defensiveness; they attested to pleasure in sexuality, and many agreed that vengeance is a value that does and should hold for our society.

Explanations that stress the causal role of distortion could also be advanced for other results obtained by us. Thus, regarding the lack of differences between male and female adolescents' levels of overall self-esteem, one could argue that members of one sex or the other are repressing their true negative feelings. Similarly, with respect to findings that girls have more negative psychological self-images, one could argue that members of one sex or the other are more open to or willing to admit negative feelings. When, however, over 50 percent of each sample of boys also attest to being "so very anxious," it is hard to know where the repression or unwillingness to admit is. On the girls' side, when 40 percent say they feel ugly and unattractive, the repression or deliberate slanting toward the positive does not seem to be the operative causal factor in producing the results obtained.

Readers are doubtless still wondering why the image of adolescents' phenomenal selves we found is so different from that ascribed to them by so many prominent psychiatrists, psychoanalysts, and clinical theorists. Would we have obtained a very different picture had we gone beyond the "superficiality" of a paper-and-pencil test and penetrated to the true inner core of feelings of these youths? Based on many years of working with normal adolescents, our answer to that question is no. When Offer began his work with normal adolescents in 1962, he had no preconceived notion that adolescents were not caught in the throes of psychological and psychosocial tumult. Only when data from many sources (including data from repeated psychiatric interviews and projective testing) converged to indicate that there was no great turmoil in adolescence did Offer conclude that this image was erroneous.

Psychoanalysts and other clinicians who have studied adolescents have, of course, observed great turmoil among them. Yet those observations were made, almost by definition, with respect to a highly select group of adolescents, that is, those adolescents who reported for treatment. It is at least plausible that the great turmoil these psychoanalysts have seen is as much a function of who they saw as of the depth and intensity of data collection methods they used. It is of course also possible that were these clinicians to observe in depth a representative sample of normal teenagers, they would uncover vast repressed or denied turmoil in that population as well. We believe, however, that the burden is on them, largely because postulating unconscious turmoil is different from demonstrating that it is, in fact, there. We have not denied the possibility of unconscious, or, at least, unacknowledged, feelings. We recognize that it is commonplace for us and other clinicians to observe that people have feelings that they would rather not admit to. Yet, there must be

## Discussion

a basis for inferring what these feelings are, something more than a bare inference from theory, to establish the existence of those feelings in an entire set of people.

Merely postulating unconscious feelings, or inferring them from the behavior of a person or a group of persons far removed from those about whom one is actually speaking, in fact may be contrasted with the work done by Sigmund Freud, the father of the investigation of unconscious feelings. When Freud (1905:125) told Dora, one of his adolescent patients, "that your love for Herr K. did not come to an end . . . but . . . has persisted down to the present day—though it is true that you are unconscious of it," Freud was not making a statement based only on theory. His conclusion instead was based on careful and laborious observation of behaviors and feelings reported by Dora herself. In the end, even Dora had to admit that the web of evidence that Freud spun—her silent acquiescence in her father's relations with Frau K., her coughing and loss of voice when Herr K. was away, her blanching when she saw her female cousin with Herr K. one day, her inability to enjoy any gifts on her birthday because he have given her none, her delay on reporting to her parents what had transpired down by the lake between her and Herr K.—irresistibly led to the conclusion that she had been and was in love with Herr K. Before Freud (1905:129) is through, Dora is helping him along. You " 'thought that your accusation [against Herr K.] might be a means of inducing him to travel to the place where you were living,' " Freud said. " 'As he actually offered to do at first,' " Dora added. Freud established Dora's feeling and convinced even Dora, who, at first, had vehemently denied her love for a man toward whom she felt only disgust when he tried to kiss her and whose face she slapped when he "proposed" down by the lake. But Freud showed Dora the unacknowledged feeling, identifying with inexorable logic its numerous manifestations.

The process Freud engaged in is far removed from making bald assertions about a group not directly studied. The word "unconscious" is not a magical incantation that allows assertions to be made about people who cannot deny them because, by definition, they are not experiencing what is being asserted. Nor is the word "unconscious" a shibboleth that allows only an anointed few access to the secret chambers of the minds of the uninformed. When addressed correctly, unconscious feelings are inferred, painfully and tentatively, from data that have been systematically collected. If psychoanalysts have data that show great unconscious turmoil among normal youth, we are eager to see it. Thus far, none has been forthcoming.

In essence, the teenagers surveyed in this book portrayed themselves in ways that bear little resemblance to the stressed, stormy, and rebellious youths described by Hall and psychoanalytic theorists. Attempts to explain away these data do not seem very promising. As far as we know, almost every researcher (Vaillant, 1977; Grinker, Grinker, and Timberlake, 1962; Masterson, 1967; Block, 1971; Rotter, Graham, Chadwick, and Yule, 1976; Davis, 1944; Hsu, 1961; Elkin and Westley, 1955; Douvan and Adelson, 1966; Gesell, Ilg, and Ames, 1956; Offer, 1969; Offer and Offer, 1975) who has studied a representative sample of normal teenagers has come to the conclusion that they are characterized by good coping and a smooth transition into adulthood.

Rosenberg's findings (1979) do stand in marked contrast to this consensus. Rosenberg found that about 85 percent of adolescents reported that their peers thought negatively of them and about 32 percent of adolescents reported high depressive affect. Rosenberg's findings seem questionable in that the term "negative" applies to three points on a four-point scale. As a result, saying peers or any other group like you "pretty much," "not very much," and "not at all" was rated negative, while saying that others like you "very much" was rated positive. High rates of negative self-perceptions on this basis may be an artifact of this scoring system. With Rosenberg's studies of depressive affect, the discrepancy between his data and ours is more obvious. One question Rosenberg asked was, "How happy would you say you are most of the time?" The response "not at all happy" represented severe depression. If the connotation of 32 percent of adolescents reporting having severe depression is that 32 percent say they are not at all happy "most of the time," then that finding contrasts sharply with our finding that about 85 percent of the adolescents we tested report being

# Discussion

happy most of the time. One explanation for this discrepancy between our and Rosenberg's data may concern the samples tested. The data Rosenberg (1979) cites was gathered in Baltimore in 1968 (see Simmons and Rosenberg, 1975) primarily among black and working-class persons. Our sample is, of course, very different demographically. Rates of depressive affect among various groups might be affected by those demographic differences.

After six years of intensive longitudinal study, Offer and Offer (1975) said "we have not found turmoil to be prevalent in our normal adolescent population." Instead, the Offers found, turmoil was only *one* way of adjusting to the challenge of adolescence—a way used by a minority of the adolescents studied. Among the majority, many adolescents coped by exerting some degree of increased self-control, and many others coped smoothly while remaining open to inner feelings and creative impulses. But among the majority, all coped effectively and without undue stress resulting from the tasks of adolescence.

In Chapter 1, we took the position that a self-image questionnaire can be viewed as a way of facilitating the sharing of subjective experiences by the persons taking it. Provided there is a good research alliance between subjects and researchers, the responses can be read as honest attempts to convey parts of the subjects' inner world (Offer, 1969). Considered in this way, the data do more than suggest that the great majority of our subjects are not in the throes of conflict and self-destructive rebellion. They also provide an index of the frequency and intensity of negative affects, rebellion, and mood swings among normal adolescents. This index provides a baseline for judging the probability that any single adolescent is within the normal range.

The data indicate, for example, that anxiety is relatively prevalent among normal teenagers. This anxiety, however, was shown to be situationally induced anxiety and not a pervasive, unceasing tenseness. Similarly, for many of the teenagers tested, relationships with parents are positive, yet this relationship also includes for many a definite sense of autonomy, a feeling that they, as adolescents, have a right to have opinions which differ from those of their parents. It appears that situationally induced anxiety and autonomy are part

92

of the normal experience of adolescence, as our data suggest, while extreme turmoil is not.

There is no question that extremely stressed, tumultuous teenagers exist. By their own self-report, many were among our group of "normal" adolescents. The only question is where to locate them on a continuum describing normal adolescent adjustment. The often-cited attitudes that such adolescents are "going through a stage," or that he or she "will outgrow this," may harm the teenager. A disturbed youngster is done no service when his mood swings are inaccurately seen as predictable, his negative affect as typical, and his extreme rebellion as understandably normal. Even more ironically, no good comes of seeing an adolescent's disturbed adjustment as confirmation of a theory about how normal adolescents feel and behave. Instead, we should ask, "How does this adolescent compare to others who cope successfully?"

Among the normals, a significant minority attest to having disturbing feelings and symptoms. About 20 percent attest to feeling empty emotionally, being confused most of the time, or hearing strange noises. These figures indicate that turmoil and maladaptation are a real part of many teenagers' lives. But while this figure is high—perhaps disturbingly so—it is useful to remember that these adolescents are far out numbered by those making a relatively smooth transition to adulthood.

## DEVELOPMENTAL PERSPECTIVE ON NORMAL ADOLESCENTS

The turmoil in the minority of normal adolescents' lives can be viewed from another perspective as well. The effective coping of the majority should not obscure the fact that youths entering adolescence find themselves confronted by tasks that are both difficult and necessary to perform. Emerging sexuality, separation from parents, preparation for and choice of occupation, and expanded peer-group relations describe the bulk, but not all, of the areas where

## Discussion

new challenges must be met. The successful coping of the majority may be more accurately understood in terms of strength and a sense of being intact than in terms of a lack of challenge and stress.

Given the number and complexity of tasks presented by adolescence, it is not surprising that some and even many youths will become deeply disturbed during this stage of life. Less clear is that, among the stages of life, adolescence is uniquely stress-inducing. It is equally plausible that adolescence is, as Erikson wrote (1959), only one of a number of "normative crises" that individuals must pass through, and that, faced with each such crisis, a number of individuals fail to cope smoothly or well. The work of Vaillant (1977), Srole and Fisher (1980), Schoeppe and Havighurst (1952), and Garber (1972) help elucidate this point. In Schoeppe and Havighurst's research, results indicated that good coping in early adolescence with respect to each of five specific tasks of adolescence correlated highly with good coping on those tasks in later adolescence, a result similar to the longitudinal findings of Offer and Offer (1975). In addition, Schoeppe and Havighurst found that, throughout the teen years, good achievement on one task tends to be associated with good achievement on other tasks. In a longitudinal study extending well into subjects' middle age, Vaillant (1977) showed that persons coping well in their early college years had better prognoses physically and emotionally than did persons who were more disturbed at that time. Garber's findings demonstrate that very disturbed adolescent patients have much poorer prognoses with respect to adult functioning than do less disturbed patients. Read together, these studies suggest that successful coping is an individual trait that manifests itself across the various life stages. Indications are that persons showing poor coping in adolescence will continue to do so during other normative crises. Srole's work on adults is relevant in that he found an incidence of severe psychiatric symptomatology comparable to that reported by our subjects. Since the incidences are comparable, this finding is consistent with the idea that individual capacities, and not the quality of a particular life stage, determine the extent of maladjustment. If adolescence is particularly and uniquely stressful, why is the prevalence of disturbance in adulthood of the same order of magnitude?

The time may have come to reexamine the contributions of clinicians to the theoretical understanding of normal adolescent development. In particular, the relevance of the work of investigators such as A. Freud, Erikson, and Blos should be questioned. A better understanding of disturbed adolescents has been firmly established in research and in clinical work. As the data from research work with normal adolescents increase, it becomes apparent that turmoil theory no longer explains the findings. This theory is simply insufficient to explain the variations of adolescent behavior, psychology, and development.

## SEX DIFFERENCES AMONG NORMAL ADOLESCENTS

### EMPIRICAL FINDINGS

The significant sex contrasts showed a consistent pattern with respect to two of the self-dimensions, the psychological self and the social self. On every psychological self-image scale, the girls reported worse feelings about themselves than did the boys; in contrast, the girls reported more positive self-image attitudes with respect to values and social sensitivity. The girls more often said they felt lonely, sad, confused, and ashamed than did the boys. Particularly notable are the decidedly negative feelings the girls expressed toward their bodies, with over 40 percent of the normal girls saying they frequently feel ugly and unattractive. At the same time, the girls were more likely to say that when a tragedy occurs to a friend, they feel sad, too. They more often asserted that they would not hurt someone just for the "heck of it," and they were more likely to deny that they would rather sit around and loaf than work.

Yet even with respect to these findings, the consistency between girls and boys is much greater than the disparity. In fact, with respect to every aspect of self-image, most girls and boys rate themselves similarly. Moreover, some intersex differences were amelio-

# Discussion

rated by age: Older girls were much more open to their sexuality than were younger girls, and were less likely to say that they had poor body images, thus bringing them closer to the levels reported by the boys.

In a general way, the findings are supported by the literature: With respect to overall self-esteem, the usual finding is that there are no significant male-female differences. Rosenberg's data (1965) are a case in point. Using his own scale with a representative New York sample, Rosenberg found almost identical self-esteem levels for boys and girls. The studies of adolescents reviewed by Wylie (1979) also show no tendency for girls to be superior to boys with respect to overall self-esteem or vice versa.

A different picture of sex differences emerges when studies that differentiate various aspects of self-esteem are considered. In this body of research, the findings repeatedly show that: (1) girls see themselves more positively than do boys with respect to interpersonal relations and sociability (Wiggins, 1973; Monge, 1973) or when their self-image is more involved with sociability (Helland, 1973); and (2) boys see themselves more positively than do girls with respect to achievement (Monge, 1973), academic aspirations (Wiggins, 1973), self-assertion (Gregory, 1977), and body image (Musa and Roach, 1973; Healey and Deblassie, 1974; Clifford, 1971). As Rosenberg (1979) points out, other self-concept differences may be found in areas other than self-esteem such as self-confidence or stability of self-concept. These differences point to girls, and white girls in particular, as having lower self-images in those areas than do boys.

The self-esteem results that require explaining can be divided into two parts: the lack of sex differences in overall self-esteem and the specific self-image areas that do reflect significant sex differences.

## THEORETICAL EXPLANATION OF THE FINDINGS

Gender-related differences in overall self-esteem are predicted by many theories. Wylie (1979) summarizes the array of variables that have been put forward to account for the supposed differences between male and female self-images. These variables range from the biological to the sociological. But in almost all of these theories, the prediction is that women will have less positive overall self-images than men. In some theories, however, which stress women's unique biological capabilities or which suggest that women possibly use a different reference group than do men or that the aspirations of women may differ from those of men (Bardwick, 1971; Weissman and Klerman, 1980), an implicit prediction is made of equal or superior self-esteem on the part of women.

Several specific questions are raised by our findings. What accounts for the better body image and higher academic and vocational aspirations of the boys? What is the source of the more positive social, moral, and affiliative orientation of the girls? And, finally, why does there seem to be a more pervasive sadness, loneliness, and confusion among the girls than among the boys?

To answer these questions, one is probably best advised to turn first to the obvious contrasts between male and female experiences during adolescence. Consider, for instance, the experience of puberty. For girls, one notable event is the onset and experience of menstruation; for boys, sexual experience is confined to growing strength and awakening sexuality. One consequence of this difference might be that the experience of bleeding is more disruptive of and more disturbing to body self-image than are the male concomitants of puberty. More likely, however, is the possibility that these experiences are shaped by traditional attitudes of Western civilization, attitudes that even in modern times lead many parents to shun menstruation as a topic of conversation with their daughters (Whisnant and Zegans, 1975) or to refer to it as the "curse." Rather different was the attitude of many American Indian groups, who, Young (1965) tells us, viewed the onset of menstruation with admiration.

Contrasting sex roles constitute another clear difference between boys and girls in our society. Despite the political and ideological influence of the women's movement, traditional sex-role orientations still seem powerful among American youths in the late 1970s and 1980. In many societies throughout the world (Harris, 1974), and certainly in Western societies, the division of labor between the sexes has led men to assume aggressive, instrumental, and dominant

97

# Discussion

roles in society while women have specialized in affiliation and nurturance (Parsons, 1964). Sexually, men have been viewed as conquerors of women who, in turn, struggled to confine their sexuality to limits prescribed by the roles of wife and mother (Weisser, 1981). In many ways, our data can be viewed as reflecting these traditional sex-role ascriptions. Pervading the boys' self-descriptions is their lack of fear, their autonomy, and their aggression. It is noteworthy that over 75 percent of the boys say they feel like leaders while the girls affirm their concern for others and traditional moral values. It is as though, in their minds, the girls are still on the side of home and hearth, while the boys are the conquerors and achievers in the larger society.

Gender-related differences in sexual attitudes are susceptible to a similar analysis. As would be expected, boys more frequently admit to sexual pleasure and inclinations than do girls. The only countervailing datum concerning developmental differences between boys and girls in this area is the fact that differences between younger and older teenagers in attitudes toward sexuality are much larger among girls than among boys. If a change is taking place in girls' sexual attitudes, it may be taking root much more strongly among older than younger teenage girls. Another explanation is that older girls are more comfortable with their bodies than are younger girls.

PHENOMENOLOGICAL INTERPRETATION

The simplest explanation of the greater prevalence of sadness and loneliness among girls is that boys react to their higher status in society and, thus, perceive better economic and social opportunities in the future than do girls. The fact that women's earnings are only two-thirds of men's earnings, and that this ratio has not changed in the last several years (U.S. Department of Labor Statistics), could contribute to such perceptions on the part of the two sexes. Given the higher aspirations of women in recent times, this perceived lack of opportunity might be especially frustrating. Generally, boys may feel more in control of their destinies and more able to achieve through personal initiative than girls do.

The fact that boys feel better about their bodies and looks generally than girls do might reflect the boys' higher esteem and status in our society. Exacerbating such a trend might be the fact that traditional affiliative and nurturing aspirations function within the open system of date and mate selection almost universally practiced in our society. Since physical attractiveness is a key variable in date and, presumably, in mate selection (Walster, et al., 1966), persons with large stakes in this area reasonably invest a great deal in being good-looking. To the extent that girls feel a strong need to be good-looking and popular and feel inadequate in these areas, they will feel insecure and disaffected, particularly with respect to their own physical selves (see Simmons and Rosenberg, 1975, for a similar explanation of findings analogous to ours in this area).

Another point is that girls may be at a disadvantage vis-a-vis boys insofar as the goals to which they are oriented are less amenable to attainment through individual effort and adaptation than are the goals to which boys are oriented. Popularity and its subsidiary goal of physical attractiveness are but two examples. Adolescents who strive for good grades can try to cope with failure by vowing to try harder next time. Similarly, the ideology surrounding sports is that practice leads to even greater attainment. By contrast, physical attractiveness is traditionally seen as more ascriptive than are academic, vocational, and athletic achievements. One can always say, "I'll do better next time" or "This is not my game, but some other game or area of achievement is." But in the realm of physical attractiveness, success or failure may be perceived to be more immutable and less open to choice than is instrumental achievement. Despite the multi-billion-dollar garment, cosmetics, and beauty salon industries, the theme may be you do the best with what you have, but you may never be able to have the best. One could speculate about the role of the media, which often portray only attractive persons as attaining romance and happiness, but in any event, the main ideas are, one, that physical beauty may be perceived more often as being difficult to achieve through individual initiative than is academic and vocational success, and, two, that physical attractiveness may be felt in many ways to be the only game in town with respect to popularity. If one feels physically unattractive, one may feel barred from being socially popular.

## Discussion

Just as cogently, adolescents may have more difficulty achieving direct feedback about how attractive they are than about how successful they are. It is hard to argue with grades or athletic scores. Popularity or unpopularity with the opposite sex is a much more uncertain criterion. We suspect, too, that, to a degree, physical attractiveness is a taboo subject in contemporary America. It is probably rare for anyone to directly tell anyone else that he or she is not attractive; there is, of course, no such reticence about failure in academics or sports. As a result, in the area of physical attractiveness, many adolescents may never quite know how they stand. Among girls, for whom this information is arguably much more important in relation to felt aspirations than it is for boys, this lack of feedback may engender notably more insecurity and self-doubt than it does among boys.

Girls may also feel more helpless with respect to popularity than do boys in a more direct way. Even in 1980, boys probably take the initiative regarding heterosexual interactions much more often than do girls. Since boys, by making increasingly more appropriate sociometric choices, can thereby adjust their social aspirations to a point where they are reasonably successful, boys have opportunity to feel good about themselves generally in this area. A girl has less ability to make this adjustment since she has less control over the selective attainment of feedback. It is always possible that a sociometric star will approach her—his failure to do so never provides the certainty that a direct rejection of a requested interaction would.

We do not want to exaggerate the extent of male-female differences in adolescent self-images. As a matter of fact, a majority of girls in both age groups do affirm that they are good-looking and proud of their bodies. But apparently, many girls do not start with this assumption. For these girls, it is possible that initial insecurity persists in the light of an inability to take control of the situation. Boys may more often assume that they are good-looking and, in case of social failure, may be more able to adjust aspirations and achievement to conform to this assumed image. Boys' instrumental aspirations may allow more room for psychological adaptation than do girls' affiliative and nurturing aspirations. Other differences in self-image may be rooted in traditional sex-role aspirations and in the dominant status of men in Western civilization, but further studies will be necessary before firm conclusions are reached.

## AGE DIFFERENCES AMONG NORMAL ADOLESCENTS

A review of the literature on age trends (see Wylie, 1979) in overall self-image supports our findings that there are no significant age differences among normal adolescents. One notable exception to this trend can be found in Rosenberg (1979), who found lower self-esteem among younger adolescents than among older adolescents. An examination of Table II in Simmons and Rosenberg (1975) shows that this effect is consistently true only for the black adolescents tested. Since we tested a sample containing a much higher percentage of whites than was contained in Rosenberg's Baltimore sample, our results, from that point of view, do not necessarily conflict with those of Rosenberg.

The repeated finding that there are no significant differences by age in self-image is surprising since contrary hypotheses are so easily generated. Wylie (1979) cites theorists who say that age gains in competence should lead to increased self-esteem; her own position is that increased exposure to reality should deflate self-esteem. A third position predicts no age differences because, in each age group, actual functioning and self-expectations are probably closely matched especially among normals.

The age differences that do occur among adolescents have to be interpreted cautiously. The trend toward better adjustment in the psychological self observed in our data makes sense insofar as it implies better self-control and body image among older as compared to younger adolescents. Better functioning with respect to peer relations and other aspects of the social self could be just as

# Discussion

easily assimilated theoretically, but the reader should keep in mind that other factors may be operative. For example, testing was done in schools, and the omission of dropouts from samples becomes increasingly important as age increases. Insofar as dropouts are expected to have lower self-esteem in general than do students who stay in school, the tendency for the older students studied to have better self-images than the younger students may be biased. The safest conclusion is that no age differences among adolescents with respect to self-image have been shown by our data. This conclusion is buttressed by the similar findings reached by most previous research.

## Cross-Decade Differences: 1970s Versus 1960s

Our data indicate that with respect to almost every self-image dimension, teenagers in the 1970s feel worse about themselves than did teenagers in the 1960s. A comparison of their self-reports suggest that 1960s adolescents were more self-confident, controlled, and more trusting of others than are 1970s adolescents. The 1960s adolescents also said more positive things about their families and reported higher ethical standards than do more contemporary adolescents.

Only with respect to sexual attitudes were there no significant differences between these groups of youths. The differences there were occurred at the item level. These differences were, respectively, that 1970s adolescents more frequently report that sexually they are "very behind," while 1960s adolescents said less often that they could enjoy a dirty joke than do their more contemporary counterparts.

When interpreting these results, it is important not to overstate the magnitude of the cross-decade differences. In the 1970s cohort and the 1960s cohort, the vast majority of adolescents affirmed positive-self-images in each sex and age group. The adolescents in both decades reported good adjustment, positive feelings, and warm relationships with their families. The cross-decade data, though, are arresting for the trend they show. Over approximately an eighteen-year period, the self-perceptions of American teenagers apparently have become decidedly less positive.

EMPIRICAL FINDINGS

Other sources also point to adolescents as being more unhappy now than those of a decade ago, though some contrary data exist. Suicide rates among teenagers have increased sharply during the last decade (Holinger and Offer, 1981A). Similarly, violence among teenagers has increased during the last decade, according to the FBI Uniform Reports Arrest Statistics, although it has leveled off in the last few years. Using self-report data, the University of Michigan's Institute for Social Research (ISR) found a general decline in the happiness among all Americans during the 1960s and late 1970s (Campbell, 1980). According to ISR, this decline was most sharp among educationally and economically advantaged subgroups and among youths.

THEORETICAL EXPLANATIONS

There are some possible theoretical explanations for cross-decade differences. Three such explanations come to mind. First, the 1960s groups grew up in a different historical period than did the 1970s groups; second, the 1960s groups were tested at a different point in time historically than were the 1970s groups; and, third, the 1960s groups were drawn from a smaller population base than were the 1970s groups. The first and second differences could be described, respectively, as generational and historical explanations. The third possibility raises the question of sampling artifacts. The third possibility seems least promising as an explanation of the results obtained. It is true that, with one exception, different high schools were tested in the 1970s and in 1980 than were tested in the 1960s. It is also true that, unlike the 1970s sample, the 1960s sample did not include rural, inner city, and upper-class youths, but the significance of these distinctions is decreased by the fact that in no age-by-sex grouping in the 1970s cohort were OSIQ total score differences significant between upper class, rural, inner city, and suburban groups. Since highly significant 1960s–1970s OSIQ total score differences summarize the most salient findings, it seems improbable that the addition of nonsuburban youths to the 1970s sample can explain

# Discussion

the result obtained. Another, more minor point is that in the 1970s cohort, a major part of the sample were Chicago suburban youths, precisely the same group sampled in the 1960s.

Generational and time effects seem to provide a better explanation of the differences. Generation is described by Mannheim (1952) in these terms: "Individuals who belong to the same generation, who share the same year of birth, are endowed, to that extent, with a common location in the historical dimension of the social process." In this theory, common historical experiences in early childhood may be particularly influential. Mannheim (1952:390) wrote, "that inventory of experience which is absorbed by infiltration from the environment in youth becomes the historically oldest stratum of consciousness, which tends to stabilize itself as the natural view of the world."

The concept of historical time is different from the concept of generation in that historical time refers to influences that affect the subjects directly at the time of testing, while generation refers to differential effects over subjects' entire lifetimes. The importance of this distinction was shown by the work of Nesselroade and Baltes (1974), who distinguished the effects of the year of birth from the time of testing in a two-year longitudinal study. Of the two variables, the authors found that the time of testing had a greater influence on adolescent personality than did the year of birth. When different cohorts—in our case, subjects born in different decades—are also tested in different decades, these effects are confounded. Group differences could be a function of the subjects' having been born in different decades and, therefore, having been subjected to different historical influences during their formative years, or the differences could be due to variations in conditions during the years in which the tests were administered. Of course, both variables could be operative simultaneously, so that explanations using these variables need not be mutually exclusive.

Regarding generational effects, those who were teenagers in the early 1960s were born in the late 1940s during the post-World War II baby boom. They grew up for the most part in the 1950s. Persons who were teenagers in the late 1970s–1980 were born between 1957 and 1967, the tail end of the same baby boom, and they grew up for the most part during the 1960s and early 1970s. It may be relevant that the 1960s generation was a relatively large cohort, and that these teenagers grew up during an era in America marked by enthusiasm and optimism.

The 1970s generation, by way of contrast, experienced the turmoil of the Viet Nam War and the antiwar movement, economic turbulence, and Watergate. Also of possible relevance is the long-term trend toward a breaking down of the traditional family, which includes the increase in the divorce rate, the number of households headed by a single parent, and the number of children growing up in single-parent households. The lower satisfaction with their families shown and the lower cohesion of their families attested to by the 1970s subjects when compared with the 1960s subjects would fit in with such a trend. This trend should be read along with Rosenberg's finding (1965) that "a somewhat larger portion of children of divorced or separated parents had low self-esteem than those whose families were intact." Wylie (1979) cites studies that make a similar point. It should also be noted that studies have connected high self-esteem in children to good parental communication (Matteson, 1974), positive interactions in the family (Laitman, 1975), and perceived parental support (Gecas, 1970). On the other hand, Wylie (1979:351) concluded:

> A survey of the literature has shown that, at present, it appears difficult if not impossible to design empirical studies which can establish clearly an antecedent-consequent relationship between family variables and the child's self-concept.

Consistent with this conclusion are the contradictory findings of Harley (1973) and Hoyte (1976) about the influence of an absent father on self-esteem. Thus, even if a change in the quality of family life that was relevant to the experiences of the 1960s and the 1970s generations did occur, there is no proof that this change would have affected self-image.

Perhaps more important with respect to lower self-esteem among contemporary teenagers when compared to 1960s teenagers is the historical time effect. Particularly important is the difference in *zeit-*

*geist* in America between the early 1960s and the late 1970s. In the early 1960s, the Viet Nam War was not yet a topic of intense public interest. Inflation and unemployment were lower. OPEC had not yet introduced its price increases, and the U.S. dollar had not weakened. Watergate was still in the future. Shifts in the legal status of adolescents that occurred over the two decades in question, which have engendered greater autonomy but also have placed greater responsibility on teenagers, had not yet taken place. All of these changes, taken together, might have resulted in lowered self-esteem among contemporary American adolescents, and perhaps even among Americans of all ages. But at best, they can only make plausible what is a surprising result.

Then, too, historical and generational effects should not be read as implying a long-term trend. In contrast to Campbell (1980), Srole's and Fischer's data (1980), which compared like-age groups, showed increases in mental well-being between 1954 and 1974. Our data and other data show a decrease in self-esteem for adolescents and other age groups between the early 1960s and the late 1970s. Srole's and Fischer's (1980) and our findings are not necessarily inconsistent. A graph showing 1954 as a low point, 1962 as a high point, and 1974–1980 somewhere in between would fit all the findings just mentioned. The point is not to assert the validity of such a graph, but to show that two data points do not necessarily constitute a trend. If the 1970s adolescents are less contented than 1960s adolescents were, no implications follow for late 1980s adolescents' self-esteem. A reversal of this seeming trend is as likely as is an exacerbation.

Up to this point, we have not talked about attitudes toward sexuality, the one area that did not show significant 1960s–1970s differences. Given the much discussed "sexual revolution," this result is surprising since it suggests that 1970s teenagers are generally no more sexually liberal than were their counterparts in the 1960s— and especially since one hypothesis we have been working with is that 1970s adolescents may have been more open about their feelings than were 1960s adolescents. If so, one would suspect that 1970s adolescents would have more freely admitted to sexually liberal attitudes than the 1960s adolescents would have. One also could argue that the 1960s subjects were sexually more conservative because, given the generally high self-esteem scores in the 1960s, these subjects' sexual attitudes scores were actually lower relative to their other self-image scores than were 1970s subjects' sexual attitudes scores relative to their other self-image scores. But since Sexual Attitudes scores do not correlate with other self-image scores (Offer, Ostrov, and Howard, 1977), Sexual Attitudes scores should not reflect a general lowering of self-image. Instead, the results seems best read literally: Teenagers today are not more liberal in their attitudes with respect to sex than they were in the 1960s. If anything—if the 1970s adolescents were more open than were the 1960s adolescents—the former group was more conservative sexually.

Instructive in this regard are the two items that did show cross-decade differences. The 1970s teenagers more often said they liked dirty jokes, but they also were more likely to see themselves as sexually way behind. Our guess is that, if nothing else, the sexual revolution has changed expectations and attitudes in the abstract. Ironically, because of the publicity given to the sexual revolution, it may be commonplace for a teenager to have the impression that other teenagers are sexually much further along than he is and to believe that other teenagers are much further along than they actually are.

## CROSS-CULTURAL DIFFERENCES

Our data are characterized more by similarities than by differences in self-image among the cultures we studied. Only with respect to the coping self were there significant differences between normal American teenagers and normal Israeli, Irish, and Australian adolescents. Otherwise, differences were confined to trends indicating somewhat more positive social selves among Americans and slightly more positive feelings about the family on the part of the adolescents from other countries.

Before commenting on cross-cultural differences, let us highlight

## Discussion

the similarities in self-image among adolescents in the cultures we studied. This consistency is particularly striking because of the possibility of different cultural interpretations of the items and, in the case of the Israelis, the possibility of mistranslations of the items. The similarities seem to indicate that OSIQ items touch on universal themes, and that these themes are ones that adolescents from very different backgrounds can respond to meaningfully. These data also imply that normality in the sense of freedom from marked turmoil and maladaptation is the norm among adolescents from many countries, and that good adaptation and relatively smooth coping is the common experience of adolescence.

Regarding the differences found, the data show that, if anything, teenagers from other countries are less rebellious than are American teenagers. Despite the very positive feelings toward their families attested to by American adolescents, those feelings tended not to be as positive as those reported by teenagers from the other three cultures sampled. American teenagers, on the other hand, tended to report somewhat more allegiance to morals and to work-related values. Americans in short, may be a bit more autonomous and less family-oriented than are adolescents from the other cultures.

The largest cross-cultural differences in our data concerned the coping self. In this area, notable contrasts existed between Irish and Australians on the one hand and the Israelis on the other, with the Americans occupying the middle ground. Especially dramatic is the positive coping described by the Israeli adolescents. The Israeli teenagers see themselves as realists who live in a hostile world that can be mastered through their own efforts. Another quality that manifests itself in the Israelis' self-image is the trust in, and reaching out toward, others. The overall picture is one of much self-confidence and trust in others in the context of realistic problems. The Israelis' confidence and trust may show the extent of human adaptability under adverse political conditions and the power of a common enemy to bring people together. The differences among the Irish, Americans, and Australians are more difficult to explain. Since the differences are indicative only of trends anyway, no attempt to explain these results will be made.

In the literature, the little evidence that exists tends to confirm our findings. Two studies discovered few differences between the self-esteem of American adolescents and that of youths from other countries (Gonzales-Tamayo, 1974; Larson, 1976) while one study found that Americans attested to being more happy (Snider, Snider and Nichols, 1968). Taken together with our data, these studies indicate that there are few cross-cultural differences in self-esteem among adolescents.

## DELINQUENT, DISTURBED, AND PHYSICALLY ILL ADOLESCENTS

While relatively little research has been done on the self-image of physically ill adolescents, many studies before ours have compared delinquent, disturbed, and normal teenagers' self-images. Therefore, we shall emphasize results obtained by others when assessing our delinquent and disturbed subjects' responses. Prior research and ours are compared first with respect to delinquent-normal and disturbed-delinquent differences in self-image. Finally, the self-images of physically ill and normal youths are contrasted.

### JUVENILE DELINQUENTS

*Others' Findings and Ours.* Our results were consistent with those of most studies of delinquents' self-images previously published. Almost every dimension measured by the OSIQ showed lower self-esteem for the delinquents than for the normal adolescents. Likewise, most past studies have shown that delinquents have lower self-esteem than do normal adolescents (Berman, 1976; Beyer, 1974; Cole, Oetting, and Hinkle, 1967; Ferguson, Freedman, and Ferguson, 1977; Walpole, 1973; Jensen, 1972; Long, Ziller, and Bankes, 1970; Norem-Hebeisen, 1975; Rathus and Seigel, 1973), although some studies found no significant differences between the two groups (see,

# Discussion

for example, Deitz, 1969), or they found differences by sex (Preston, 1967; Gold and Mann, 1972).

At the item level, our results indicated that the delinquents we studied were much more hostile, unhappy, suspicious, confused, empty, ashamed, and pessimistic than were the normals; delinquents' reports about their families were especially negative. At the same time, the delinquents reported having more positive feelings about their physical attractiveness than did the normals, and attested to owing as much allegiance to the work ethic as did normals. More surprisingly, the delinquents also perceived themselves as having as much self-control as did the normals.

Earlier work tends to confirm most of these findings as well. Thus, various studies indicate that delinquent-normal differences may be especially pronounced in the area of family relations or school functioning (Atkins, 1974; Evans, 1977) or in specific dimensions of self-appraisal, such as being hostile toward, or not caring about, others (Gottuso, 1974). Non-self-image data indicate delinquents are more likely to be unhappy, suspicious, restless, and defensive than are nondelinquents (see, for example, Schachtel, 1950; Conger and Miller, 1966; Healy and Bronner, 1936). The often-reported finding that delinquents are behaviorally more impulsive than are nondelinquents (Porteus, 1945; Offer, Marohn and Ostrov, 1979) is less consistent with results we obtained and therefore will warrant a somewhat more detailed discussion later.

*Implications of These Findings.* Many of the findings test sociological and psychological theories about the etiology of delinquent behavior. Our sample of delinquents may be a special one, in that many of the subjects were institutionalized for emotional problems as well as delinquency and may differ from those likely to be found in correctional settings or in the community. The fact that our findings are consistent with past research, however, implies that they pertain to a great many, not a small subset, of juvenile delinquents. It seems fair to note that most sociological and economic theorists would not predict that delinquents have poorer self-images than nondelinquents. It is not clear that a delinquent who uses an illegitimate means to a legitimate end (Merton, 1957), behaves in a way approved

110

by his subculture but not by the dominant culture (Miller, 1958), or makes a rational economic decision to commit a crime in light of the risk of getting caught (Short and Strodtbeck, 1965), would be likely to report having low self-esteem.

One might think that psychologists, more than sociologists, would be likely to predict poorer self-esteem among delinquents than among normals. But this conclusion might not be correct for many psycho-analytic theorists, most of whom stress the role of unconscious con-flict in causing delinquency. As a case in point, consider Aichhorn (1948), probably the most authoritative psychoanalytic writer on the subject of delinquency. The principal distinction Aichhorn made was between neurotic and dyssocial delinquents. According to this theory, the neurotic suffers from unconscious conflict that he resolves through antisocial behavior while the dyssocial delinquent can be a product of parental overindulgence and lack of restraint. In neither case need self-esteem be especially low. The neurotic denies his conflict, and he might predictably exaggerate his self-worth in a defensive way. The dyssocial delinquent, if overindulged, might be likely, for that reason, to overevaluate himself.

Low delinquent self-esteem, in other words, is not a given. One could argue that the low self-esteem scores we and others obtained are not phenomenologically valid, a possibility we shall come to shortly. But, if our findings are accepted, low delinquent self-esteem could question the validity of a number of theories of delinquent behavior.

Other theories are more compatible with our data. From a socio-logical view, it is possible that low self-esteem might be an incidental result of certain more directly causative social forces. An example might be Shaw and McKay's theory (1969) of delinquent behavior, in which lack of community stability and a resulting sense of anomie are seen as prime causes of delinquency. Shaw and McKay's theory is also associated with a lack of good adult role models and diminished economic opportunity. All of these factors could easily lead to poor self-esteem among those affected by them. Another possibility is that put forward by Reckless, Dinitz, and Murray (1956), who wrote extensively about the role of poor self-esteem in generating delin-

# Discussion

quent behavior. If poor self-esteem differentially causes delinquent behavior, it would have to be true that delinquents generally have poor self-esteem.

Similarly, in contrast to many sociological and psychoanalytic theorists, investigators who emphasize the etiological role of variables such as the happiness of the parents' marriage (Nye, 1958), the cohesiveness and emotional atmosphere of the home (McCord, McCord, and Zola, 1959), and the nature of parental discipline (Glueck and Glueck, 1950; McCord, McCord, and Zola, 1959) would predict many of the details of the specific delinquent self-image pattern that emerged from our data. That delinquents would be sad, confused, and pessimistic on the one hand and suspicious, hostile, and defensive on the other is predictable from the emotionally impoverished and inconsistent family backgrounds that many delinquents apparently have experienced. The fact that in two longitudinal studies (McCord, McCord, and Zola, 1959; Glueck, 1959), lack of family cohesiveness was a major predictor of future delinquency strengthens the role of family variables still more. These studies tend to rule out any argument that bad family relations are merely a short-term effect that correlates only with parents' not wanting to, or not being able to, prevent their children from being labeled as delinquent. Similarly, they tend to rebut the argument that defiance and hostility toward the family are a product of the labeling process itself, that they are part of a generalized anger toward all authority. Instead, the indications are that disharmonious family relations are problems of long standing.

The issue of delinquents' self-control is more difficult to explain. Most investigators find delinquents to be behaviorally more impulsive than are normals. Yet, by their own report in our data, delinquents appear to be only slightly more impulsive than normals. To explain this discrepancy, one could speculate that loss of control is more difficult for delinquents to admit to themselves than is unhappiness or conflict with their families (Marohn, Offer, and Ostrov, 1971). These results, in other words, most likely are due to an effort on the part of many delinquents to preserve a part of their self-images that is of particular concern to them: the ability to stay in control of the situation. Apparently, delinquents are more willing to admit to loneliness and confusion than to loss of self-control, while not hesitating to affirm their hostility and their pride in their physical appearance.

Also surprising is the fact that the delinquents scored significantly lower on the psychopathology scale than did not only the normal subjects but the disturbed subjects. At the item level, the delinquents specifically stated more often than did the normals and the disturbed that they were confused, felt empty emotionally, and had strange feelings upon entering a new room. One explanation may be that the delinquent group contained many psychiatrically disturbed subjects, perhaps even more subjects who were more disturbed than those in the disturbed groups. If present, this bias in our sample might be related to a national trend toward institutionalizing fewer delinquents than in the past, so that those that are institutionalized are among the more serious offenders (see Murray, Thomson, and Israel, 1978, for statistics that confirm these trends in Illinois with respect to arrest rates prior to institutionalization from 1974 to 1977). Many delinquents are being diverted from penal settings to psychiatric facilities designed to treat offenders. These youths are both severely disturbed psychiatrically and seriously delinquent. Since many of the delinquents we tested were institutionalized in in-patient programs for disturbed delinquents, our findings may reflect the presence of a greater preponderance of disturbed adolescents than might be found in correctional settings generally.

The fact that delinquents attested to a high level of psychopathology raises another issue as well. It could be contended that delinquents' self-image scores are particularly prone to distortion. For example, delinquents might be less willing than are most subjects to say they feel good about themselves when they do not, thus accounting, in a non-phenomenological way, for delinquents' low self-esteem scores. This kind of argument, though, entirely fails to encompass the pattern of self-image responses obtained from the delinquents. In actuality, low overall self-esteem was found in the context of relatively high affirmations of certain aspects of self-image, such as positive body image. No hypothesis using across-the-board response tendencies could adequately account for these data.

In general, we believe that in the context of ongoing, negative

# Discussion

family experiences, delinquents coped using a hostile, suspicious withdrawal that left them feeling at the same time autonomous, proud, sad, confused, and empty. It may be especially important for these delinquents to believe they are in control of themselves even when their actions imply that they are not. In contrast to what might be predicted using certain sociological and psychological theories, the delinquents we studied felt and were willing to admit to psychological pain experienced amidst a rebellious, autonomous interpersonal stance.

## PSYCHIATRICALLY DISTURBED ADOLESCENTS

In our study, the disturbed adolescents, while significantly lower than the normals in overall self-esteem, were actually higher than the normals on two scales: Impulse Control and Morals. The problems of disturbed teenagers were concentrated in the realm of subjective feelings and interpersonal relationships: Disturbed affect, pessimism, poor body image, and difficulty relating to peers were particular problems for these youths. As did the delinquents, these youths reported that unsatisfactory relationships and negative feelings characterized their family backgrounds. At the same time, while the disturbed youths did not report more psychopathology than did the delinquents, the disturbed teenagers did see themselves as less active copers, more concerned about others' opinions, and less attractive heterosexually than did the delinquents. As might be expected, of the two groups, it was the disturbed group that scored higher on the Morals and Impulse Control scales.

That disturbed youths would have low self-esteem is not surprising. While grandiose schizophrenics or manics might report high self-esteem, most troubled youths ordinarily would be expected not to feel particularly good about themselves. Indeed, a positive self-image was described as among the more important aspects of mental health by the vast majority of psychotherapists surveyed in a national sample (Goldman and Mendelsohn, 1969), and unacceptable feelings about oneself have been assigned a critical role in emotional disturbance in virtually every major theory of psychopathology. Consistent with this position are our findings and those of many other investigators

(Preston, 1967; Shafiabady, 1975; Gildston, 1967; Rosenberg, 1965; Coopersmith, 1967; and Wylie, 1979). Hauser (1976) also found that normal adolescents' self-images are better integrated structurally than are the self-images of disturbed adolescents.

The relatively high degree of control and morality shown by the disturbed youths might be viewed as part of their syndrome. In contrast to the delinquents, we can speculate, poor family backgrounds led these youths not to rebellion but to deep self-doubts and emotional turmoil. Feeling worse about their bodies and feeling sadder, lonelier, and more rejected by their parents than the delinquents do, the disturbed subjects presumably still did not break the law. An overriding sense of control and morality might account for this. One might say that theirs was the way not of renunciation of the world of normals, but instead a feeling of inability to live up to it.

PHYSICALLY ILL ADOLESCENTS

Fewer studies describe the self-image of physically ill adolescents than describe that of delinquent or disturbed youngsters, and at the time of this writing, no discernible trend can be gleaned from the studies that do exist. Two such studies show, respectively, that disabled groups have (McFern, 1974) and do not have (Collier, 1969) more negative self-images than do normal groups. Another study (Meissner, Thoreson, and Butler, 1967) found that female disabled youths had poorer self-images than did normals, but this did not hold for males. The disparity of these findings suggests that much more work needs to be done regarding the self-images of physically ill adolescents.

Our data show that in many areas the physically ill group was similar to the normals. These areas include self control, morals, work ethics, feelings toward families, and optimism about the future. In contrast, the physically ill youths more often reported negative affects such as despondency, loneliness, and feelings of inadequacy than did the normal teenagers. The physically ill also more frequently said negative things about their bodies, their ability to make or keep friends, and their contribution to the family than did the

## Discussion

normals. The most dramatic of the differences between the groups were their respective responses to the Sexual Attitudes scale. Of all the groups we studied, the physically ill were by far the most conservative in their sexual attitudes. Compared to the normals in particular, they rejected the importance of sex while admitting they felt behind and unattractive heterosexually. Impressive, too, in its own way, is the physically ill adolescents' apparent adaptation to their sexual needs. For youths who feel unattractive and sexually behind, and who in most cases can probably do little about it, rejecting sex is a form of adaptive behavior. Perhaps it is denial, but the alternative, longing for the unattainable, is probably much more painful and despair-inducing.

It is to be expected that these youths, most of whom are suffering from severe debilitating illnesses, feel vocationally more inadequate, more despondent, more tense, and less attractive than do normals. Equally understandable is their loneliness, their isolation, and their feeling that they are a burden to their family. All the more impressive, therefore, is their optimism about the future and their continued affirmation of work values and family relationships.

The physically ill teenagers' self-images can be read as if they are a validation of the phenomenological accuracy of the OSIQ. Where the physically ill youths differ from normals is where they might be expected to differ.

## SUMMARY

The data reviewed reveal a great deal about the phenomenology of self-perceptions of adolescents grouped by age, gender, decade of testing, country of origin, and psychosocial status. The results reveal that normal adolescents are not in the throes of turmoil. The vast majority function well, enjoy good relationships with their families and friends, and accept the values of the larger society. In addition, most report having adapted without undue conflict to the bodily changes and emerging sexuality brought on by puberty.

The only notable symptom among the normals was a situation-specific anxiety, which normal adolescents can handle without undue trauma (Offer, 1969).

While age differences in the normal sample were not notable, sex differences were. Girls felt worse about their bodies, less open to sexual feelings, and more lonely or sad than did boys. The girls had more positive attitudes in the areas of affiliation and morality. These results can be explained primarily in terms of traditional sex roles that exercise their influence on an orientation to certain areas such as individual achievement and interpersonal cohesiveness.

Major differences were also found between normal adolescents of the 1960s and those of the 1970s and 1980. Almost all differences, our data indicate, point to adolescents' great self-esteem during the 1960s. The main hypothesis available to explain these data was that the formative experiences, or the *zeitgeist,* of the 1960s cohort were more conducive to positive self-esteem than were the analogous experiences of the 1970s group.

Cross-cultural differences generally were small and suggestive of the fact that adolescence may have universal characteristics in Western culture. A core of that universal experience is smooth coping.

Contrasts between normal, delinquent, psychiatrically disturbed, and physically ill youths were significant in many areas. The specific pattern of delinquent as opposed to normal self-image seems to fit best a family-oriented etiological model. This model, for instance, can explain comfortably the defiance, unhappiness, and negative family attitudes of many delinquents whereas sociological or psychoanalytic theories cannot easily do so. The high degree of self-control and morality attested to by the psychiatrically disturbed subjects in comparison to the delinquents may explain their presumably lower rates of delinquency. These youths feel as badly about their families as do the delinquents. But instead of overt rebellion and hostility, they are filled with self-doubt and pessimism.

The self-images of physically ill youths demonstrate the phenomenological authenticity of the OSIQ while providing testimony regarding human adaptability. These youths express their sadness, isolation, and negative feelings about their physical well-being, yet they retain

## Discussion

a sense of optimism and commitment to values and family. With regard to sexual attitudes, the physically ill downplay the importance of something they feel they cannot yet attain.

These results present a picture of how youths from a variety of backgrounds and statuses see themselves. In the next chapter the implications of these data will be related to theories of adolescent development, understanding various kinds of adolescents, and the place of the adolescent in an adult world.

# 9

# ADOLESCENTS IN AN ADULT WORLD

IN THIS CHAPTER, we discuss the view of adolescence held by adults in our culture. We explore the extent to which developmental theories can incorporate the findings presented in this volume. Adolescents traditionally have served as a near-perfect projective device for their elders. It seems to us that a closer scrutiny of adolescence viewed by adolescents will help adults to change their stereotypic view of teenagers. It will also help those adolescents who desperately need mental health care.

## ADOLESCENTS AS VIEWED BY ADULTS

To most adults, adolescence is a period when persons who already have stable personality characteristics cope with challenges in cognitive, affective, and social areas of functioning. In this view, adolescents will go on to meet other challenges in life with a degree of success that is roughly proportional to that which they exhibited during adolescence. Adolescents will change, yet in a sense very much remain the same.

Another way to conceptualize adolescence is as an "in-between stage" of life characterized primarily by a degree of disruption and change that occurs at no other time. Seen this way, adolescence is simply a transitional stage, a time of life when behaviors reflect less the person than the painful developmental change that that person is undergoing. This conceptualization probably typifies the view of adolescence held by most mental health professionals. Yet much evidence exists that militates against this view.

For example, disruption and change are hardly unique to adolescence. For that reason, conceptualizing adolescence as one of the very few transitional stages in the life cycle is misleading. Every stage of life brings new challenges and opportunities. These lead to changes that are a function of successes or failures during that stage and are incorporated into the basic personality structure. Adolescence is probably no more transitional than the "mid-life crises," "menopausal crises," "retirement crises," and so on, that adults are thought to go through. No one has suggested that we call these adult stages transitional. Why do many theorists consider only adolescence transitional, especially when doing so tends to have possible perjorative connotations and also serves to minimize the stable characteristics of adolescence?

A possible explanation in the case of psychoanalysts is that classical psychoanalytic theory (Freudian) basically has explained development in terms of the resolution of past conflicts. According to this theory, the adolescent has to rework the conflicts that were repressed during latency and that reemerge. This is, in part, why the psychoanalyst Blos (1962) called adolescence the second individuation stage. According to Blos, adolescents re-experience their past conflicts and have a chance to really resolve them. This resolution can be reached through a major crisis in behavior with serious repercussions in affect, cognition, and other internal states. The underlying theoretical premise is that the present is predetermined by what took place in the past.

Events in each person's past, we agree, have a differential impact on present functioning and feelings. What is less clear is whether it is always necessary to recreate the past before developmental advancement can take place. In normal as contrasted to neurotic development it is less likely that early relationships emerge and continuously disrupt the present functioning of the individual. In the case of normals, conflicts and tasks specific to each developmental stage are coped with slowly, allowing for stability of personality configuration. Social and cultural structures also help the individual to maintain emotional equilibrium. Normal adolescents generally are hopeful, positive, and future oriented. Hence, the past is of relatively less significance to normals than it is to psychiatrically disturbed adolescents.

A variety of developmental theories exist that pertain to the psychological characteristics of adolescence (for example, Stone and Church, 1979; Weiner, 1970; Conger, 1975; Newman and Newman, 1979; and Blos, 1962). Differences in tone among these theories should not obscure important theoretical differences among the various systems. For example, Piaget (1968) wrote about the adolescent as a philosopher who ponders his place in the world and struggles with his attempts to make sense of life. In contrast, psychoanalysts (A. Freud, 1946; H. Deutsch, 1967; Erikson, 1959) describe the adolescent as if he were an ascetic, introspective, idealistic person who challenges the "truths" of his elders. The psychoanalysts view emotional turmoil as an essential element of growing up.

Our data support none of these interpretations. We believe, instead, that each theory explains aspects of the psychology of certain adolescents, but that none is universal enough to explain the psychology of adolescence in general. Indeed, it would seem that the very diversity of adult views on adolescence illustrates why a great deal of empirical data are still needed to help develop a sound theory.

One problem with present theories is that they tend to consist of expectations that adults have of adolescents, not the experience of adolescents themselves. As we have seen, data collected directly from normal adolescents are often significantly different from what many adults assume teenagers feel about themselves. Adolescence, as we have noted, is the world's most perfect projective device for adults. Adults' own fears and urges may interfere with their ability to correctly perceive what teenagers are really like. Leftover unful-

## Discussion

filled dreams and fantasies are easily projected onto adolescents and may also interfere with adults' understanding. Many adults hold on to the hope that their adolescent children will achieve what they have not been able to. Others fear that their children will surpass them. The vigor, strength, beauty, and sexual attractiveness of the growing adolescent may also threaten the adult. From a different perspective, the growing young represent to adults, the adults' own inevitable demise. In addition, the adult may need to put some distance between himself and his young offspring to help prevent his acting upon his own, mostly unconscious, sexual impulses. As Freud speculated in *Totem and Taboo* (1913), the conflict between the generations is a continuous one, although it represents itself in a variety of forms.

Many adults also expect that peers will have a stronger influence on their adolescent children than their own peers have on the adults themselves. When children enter adolescence, the physical and emotional power that the parents had over them is diminished considerably. Parents may realize at that time that their children have not only begun the separation process, but that they are beginning to be influenced by peers—an influence that parents tend to overemphasize. The parents then use the peer group as an externalized object and influence that provides a reference group for expressions of dissatisfaction with their offspring. Delinquency, in particular, is often ascribed to peer influences by parents in a desperate attempt to avoid recognizing the child's role and, by implication, the parents' own role in the etiology of the child's behavior.

Contributing to adults' incorrect perception of teenagers is the fact that parents are continuously being advised by professionals that adolescents are difficult beings. Anna Freud (1958:276) has stated: "There are few situations in life which are more difficult to cope with than our adolescent son or daughter during the attempt to liberate themselves." More recently, Rabichow and Sklansky (1980) agreed with the above statement. These statements portray how leading psychoanalysts characterize adolescence.

Consistent with this pessimistic view of adolescence is the publicity given to the idea that youth have been exhibiting ever-increasing violence. For years social and behavioral scientists have warned us that violence among the young is on the increase. They maintain that homicide and other violent crimes have increased at alarming rates since World War II.

Is there any solid basis of fact for this widespread belief that, in the years since World War II, there has been considerable increase in juvenile delinquency? Morris and Hawkins (1970:149) wrote: "A hundred years ago whole areas of New York were held in the grasp of street gangs like the Hudson Dusters, The Forty Thieves, etc. These gangs fought savage battles in the streets. A death toll of 15 or 20 was not uncommon. Even the police feared to enter some neighborhoods." Today, a death toll of one or two provokes nation-wide alarm and prolonged and agonized debate.

In fact, rates of violent crimes by adolescents have fluctuated in the past fifty years. If we look only at a part of the curve, that is, a few years at a time, we miss the broader (and more correct) picture. For example, it has been demonstrated that violent crimes committed by adolescents steadily increased during the 1960s and early 1970s (Uniform Crime Reports, F.B.I.). Easy explanations have been sought and found. In the late 1970s, however, violent crimes performed by adolescents actually decreased. Holinger (1980) has stated another salient point:

> Contrary to popular opinion, the mortality rate from violent deaths has not increased but, rather, has tended to decrease, with fluctuations similar to those of suicide rates. Thus the emergence of violent deaths as a leading cause of mortality is due to a decrease in the importance of other causes rather than to an increase in the rate of violent death [for individuals between one and thirty-nine years of age].

Another example concerns suicide. The rate of suicide among white middle-class adolescents continuously increased between 1956 and 1976 (Holinger and Offer, 1981A). Explanations have focused on social factors such as the breakdown of the nuclear family, the unethical conduct of elected officials, and threats of nuclear war. These explanations fall short scientifically when, without any apparent change in the social field, the suicide rate among the young decreases (Holinger and Offer, 1981B).

We have offered an empathic ecological explanation of these

## Discussion

data. We examined the suicide rate among adolescents over the past forty-two years and found a significant positive correlation between adolescent suicide rates, and changes in the proportion of adolescents in the total population of the United States (Holinger and Offer, 1981B). These data indicate that the adolescent suicide rate reacts significantly to fluctuations in population size or the density of adolescents in society. An increase in adolescent population may intensify a sense of isolation and increase the tendency to suicide: It may be more difficult for an adolescent to gain a sense of self-worth and to find friends in the large impersonal high schools of today than in the smaller schools of the past. A disturbed, lonely, emotionally depleted, depressed adolescent may look around him and see most of his peers functioning relatively well, sharpening his awareness of his personal problems and increasing his loneliness and isolation. Seeing so many seemingly well-functioning peers may also lower his already low and excessively vulnerable self-esteem with the consequent sense of hopelessness, resulting in a suicide attempt or suicide.

The population of adolescents has decreased since 1976, and it was our prediction that the suicide rate among adolescents would decrease. Initial examination of statistics on adolescent suicide rate, as well as the number of adolescents in the population for the years 1978 and 1979, have supported our hypothesis. The interested reader is referred to the various volumes of *Vital Statistics of the United States* for the background data on suicide rates. A more comprehensive comparison is made in Holinger and Offer (1981B). The hypothesis we advanced, however, is less important than the fact of fluctuation and the absence of facile explanations for these fluctuations.

The preponderance of evidence (Holinger, 1980) indicates that the percentage of violent deaths among adolescents by suicide, homicide, and accident has stayed constant over the past eighty years. Yet few adults are aware of this fact or choose to let it influence their view of adolescents. They prefer, instead, to imbue adolescents with extreme behavioral characteristics.

An ironic counterpart to the pessimistic view of teenagers is the portrayal of adolescents as misunderstood saviors of mankind (see,

124

for example, Cox Commission Report, 1968). In this view, adolescents not only offer hope, but are much more in tune with changing times. Margaret Mead (1970:77–78) stated that the world has changed so much as to preclude any communication between the generations:

> Today, nowhere in the world are there elders who know what the children know, no matter how remote and simple the societies are in which the children live. In the past there were always some elders who knew more than any children in terms of their experience of having grown up within a cultural system. Today there are none. It is not only that parents are no longer guides, whether one seeks them in one's own country or abroad. There are no elders who know what those who have been reared within the last twenty years know about the world into which they were born. . . . The elders are separated from them by the fact that they, too, are a strangely isolated generation. No generation has ever known, experienced, and incorporated such rapid changes, watched the sources of power, the means of communication, the definition of humanity, the limits of their explorable universe, the certainties of a known and limited world, the fundamental imperatives of life and death—all change before their eyes. They know more about change than any generation has ever known and so stand, over, against, and vastly alienated, from the young, who by the very nature of their position, have had to reject their elders' past.

By comparison, Kett (1977) stressed that, all things considered, circumstances between the generations were not so different in the past. If anything, the relationship between the generations is more intimate now than it ever was. People are more involved with, and cognizant of, each others' needs, feelings, and welfare than they have ever been before.

It would appear that to have a better understanding of adolescents, adults must stop foisting their fears, dreams, fantasies, and wishes on them. Adults must learn to listen empathically to adolescents' descriptions of their internal and external worlds. They must compare the description of one adolescent population to another, and, whenever possible, consider the long-range perspective when evaluating the young. Finally, adults must accept phenomenological data on adolescence and use them to formulate their theories.

# Discussion

## IMPLICATIONS FOR PARENTS AND PROFESSIONALS

In a recent study (Offer, Ostrov, and Howard, 1981A), mental health professionals (psychiatrists, psychologists, and social workers) were asked to complete the OSIQ the way they believed a normal, mentally healthy adolescent would complete it. In seven out of ten scales, the mental health professionals described the normal adolescent as significantly more disturbed than the normal adolescent viewed himself or herself. The professionals even saw the normal adolescent as having more problems than were reported by samples of either psychiatrically disturbed or delinquent adolescents. These results highlight the problems that mental health professionals have in conceptualizing the self-image of normal, mentally healthy individuals. Mental health professionals have not yet caught up conceptually with the empirical data, and unless a major effort is made to study normal adolescent development, these workers will continue to echo the words of Anna Freud (1958:275), who stated that "to be normal during the adolescent period is by itself abnormal."

So persistent are mental health professionals and theorists in upholding this view of adolescence that we must wonder what advantages it holds for them. A possible advantage to viewing normal adolescents as psychopathological is that clinicians may feel more comfortable working with psychiatrically disturbed individuals than with normal adolescents. Clinicians have to have a high tolerance for deviance in order to be able to treat severely disturbed individuals successfully. Having that tolerance may predispose one to use it in an effort to capitalize on the strengths one has.

Another advantage may be the need to maintain a certain social construction of reality. Adelson and Doehrman (1980:113–14) described this phenomenon:

When the psychodynamic theorist turns away from the study of the disturbed, and looks about him for examples of "normality," his eye is likely to fall on those most near and dear—his own children and those of his friends and neighbors, or—if he is connected to a university—his students. In short he will tend to understand the "ordinary" adolescent

126

through the observation of a narrow social enclave, one which tends to emphasize for its youngsters the values of "expressiveness" (as against inner restraint), of "rebelliousness" (as against conformity), and of adversarial indignation (as against the acceptance of social givens). Hence, we find a continuing failure to give sufficient weight to those habitual strategies of coping found among many and perhaps most adolescents—those which involve ego restriction, and an identification with the values and standards of the family and dominant social institutions. The emphasis, instead, is given to traits and qualities well-represented in the upper-middle class—the intellectualizing strategy being one example, and another, the stress placed upon ideals, values, and the taking of moral positions on social issues. The issue here is not the importance of these qualities for understanding the common adolescent experiences of the youngsters of modernity; rather, it is the ready tendency to universalize what is specific to a particular social cadre in a particular historical era. One well-known psychoanalyst has written that "developing a social conscience is a universal need" (Solnit, 1972). One may doubt that it is a need; one may be certain that it is not universal. In the sense in which it is employed, "social conscience" is an attitude rare and unknown during most of human history and throughout most of the world today. But it is an attitude frequently seen in the morally uneasy youngsters of a moralizing class in a historically moralistic nation—and it is those youngsters, that class, that nation which provide the social and historical milieu occupied by most writers in the psychodynamic tradition. In the absence of methods which would expose them to more diverse strata, the result is a social and historical parochialism.

Many mental health professionals fail to distinguish between acting out based on internal psychological conflicts and rebellion for a "just cause." The young delinquent, for example, may be telling us that he has more problems vis-a-vis his family than with his own sexuality or aggression. So be it. Let us begin the long road of helping the delinquent in need of professional help by working with his feelings toward his family. Let us not tell him what we believe his "real" or "deep seated" problem is.

Diagnostic work with adolescents has always been difficult (Masterson, 1967). Part of the difficulty has been to distinguish serious psychopathology from mild crisis. Adolescents in the midst of severe identity crisis or emotional turmoil are not just experiencing a part of normal growing up. Such adolescents and their parents are not helped when experts tell them not to worry about their problems

# Discussion

because the problems are a normal part of adolescence that will disappear with time. The clinician needs to be able to diagnose what is presented to him, yet he can do this only when he has a broader perspective on the varieties of adolescent behavior that includes a realistic view of normal adolescents. Most important, the clinician needs to realize that adolescents are primarily individuals and not merely personifications of a certain stage of development. If these facts are kept in mind, clinicians will be able to isolate adolescents' problems primarily along individual developmental lines rather than dwelling on ill-founded impressions of the "necessities of their age."

Throughout this book, we have focused on adolescents' own views of their psychological worlds. By studying normal youths, we created a baseline to guide us in our evaluation and treatment of their disturbed peers. This baseline can be used to identify the specific problems that deviant adolescents believe they have, and can enhance our ability to communicate with and to help these deviant youngsters. Theories concerning adolescent development are of little value if they do not include the adolescents' view of himself and his world.

We stressed that knowing another human being is always a relative matter. The goals of the person seeking to know play a decisive role in determining what is learned. For example, if an adult seeks to learn about an adolescent for the adult's own purposes only, then knowing the adolescent will mean enhancing and furthering the adult's goals, which may include controlling an adolescent or using him as a projective device. Control might not require any knowledge of adolescents' self-feelings and perceptions; and projection is facilitated by not being aware of how the adolescent actually feels. If, instead, the adult seeks to know the adolescent as a way to help the adolescent more effectively direct his own life, or as a way of knowing the adolescent as a goal in itself, then knowledge of that adolescent's self-feelings is essential.

We set out to learn what teenagers think and feel about themselves in five areas—Psychological, Social, Familial, Sexual, and Coping. To do so we used no projective tests, no hidden cameras, and no experimental manipulations. We simply asked the teenagers, in effect, to tell us about themselves. We believe that these thousands of adolescents, whom we saw in many different settings, had enough integrity, interest, cognitive ability, and sense of alliance with us to fill out our questionnaire accurately and diligently in almost all cases. This book stands as evidence for the idea that adolescents, when approached as persons and listened to as persons, can and will share a great deal of their subjective feelings.

Adolescents are molded by a combination of genetic predisposition; chance experiences in life; and interactions with family, culture, and social environment. If they grow up relatively unscathed by external events, their tendency is to mirror in their adulthood their parents' behavior, affective range, and cognitive processes.

Adults must recognize that adolescents are participants in the human condition. Just as adults endure suffering, psychological trauma, and tragedy, so do adolescents. Just as adults have conflicts, problems, and at times, exhibit disruptive behaviors, so do adolescents. But just as adults have the potential for being happy (see for example, Bradburn, 1969), so do adolescents. Given a relatively conflict-free development, a relatively good biological background, and positive relationships with others, adolescents have the same potential for being happy as do adults. Like adults, adolescents have the potential to relate well and responsibly to their peers and to other persons who may be significant to them, and to cope well with their external and internal environments.

Throughout the ages, adults have created a "generation gap" by systematically distorting the adolescent experience. This has clearly been a disservice to normal teenagers, since distortion forestalls effective communication. But it is also a disservice to deviant and disturbed teenagers, since they are denied needed help by adults who blithely assert that adolescents are just "going through a stage." Our message is simple. Teenagers are persons—persons whose feelings, thoughts and behaviors are as varied and rich as those of adults. The portrait of the adolescent is best drawn by him/herself.

PART

# FOUR

## Appendices

# APPENDIX A

The Construction of the Offer Self-Image
Questionnaire (OSIQ)
for Adolescents

## THE OBJECTIVE STUDY OF SELF

THE OSIQ was developed in 1962 as a means of gathering data about adolescents' phenomenal selves. The construct "phenomenal self" has been measured in a great number of ways (Wylie, 1974), which include assessments of people who know the subject, ratings of interviews with the subject, ratings of the subject's responses to projective tests, ratings of responses to incomplete sentences, and scores derived from having the subject fill out structured questionnaires. Helpful as each of these methods is, no one method is superior to the others (Wylie, 1971). The advantages and disadvantages of each method depend on the purposes and circumstances of the particular inquiry, but there are some special advantages that made us settle on the structured questionnaire format.

Structured self-image questionnaires such as the Bills (Bills, Vance, and McLean, 1951), the Tennessee Self-Concept Scale (Fitts, 1965), and the Offer (Offer, Ostrov, and Howard, 1977) consist of a series of statements that a subject is asked to confirm or disconfirm. The most important advantages of the questionnaire are its use of standard questions and the limited number of response alternatives that are available to the subject. Since each subject receives the same set of items in the same format, variations due to stimuli on the test are minimized. As a result, the response variability that does occur can be attributed mainly to intersubject differences, which is precisely the intended target of measurement.

The structured response format assures reliable scoring by precluding problems of interrater reliability and facilitating studies of internal consistency and stability. Internal consistency refers to testing the consistency of responses within different scales of the test; stability results from giving the test, or alternate versions of it, to the same subjects at two or more different times.

The ability to evaluate reliability accurately helps to insure the attainment of reliability since a test constructor can use feedback from reliability studies to modify the instrument (Offer and Howard, 1972). Good reliability results in the possibility of effectively testing concurrent and predictive validity. If reliability is poor, the result will be a failure to find predicted correlations that should be attributed to error or "noise" in the test. Moreover, since structured tests always tap a limited number of dimensions, whether by design or through the selection of a limited number of items, and they do so in easily quantifiable ways, hypotheses relating aspects of the self to other measures are easily tested. As a result of all these considerations, structured questionnaires are particularly useful as scientific tools for measuring the self.

The weaknesses of the structured self-image questionnaire approach are that it forces subjects to respond to a given set of items and to no others, and that it usually weights items according to an *a priori* scale. Theoretically, the structured test could omit items that are, for any given subject, the most salient aspects of his self-image. But the stimulus presented to the adolescents studied is identical and allows for meaningful individual and group comparisons.

All the alternatives to the use of structured questionnaires have weaknesses and strengths. The results obtained by the various approaches to the measurements of self-concept have been similar (Wylie, 1971).

## Development of the Offer Self-Image Questionnaire

Items were written to cover eleven areas of an adolescent's life that were believed, on the basis of theoretical propositions, clinical experience, and a review of empirical findings, to be important to the psychological life of the adolescent. The eleven areas and the number of items originally included for each are:

| Scale | Title | Number of Items |
|---|---|---|
| 1 | Impulse Control | 10 |
| 2 | Emotional Tone | 10 |
| 3 | Body and Self-Image | 10 |
| 4 | Social Relationships | 10 |
| 5 | Morals | 10 |
| 6 | Sexual Attitudes | 10 |
| 7 | Family Relationships | 20 |
| 8 | Mastery of the External World | 10 |
| 9 | Vocational and Educational Goals | 10 |
| 10 | Psychopathology | 15 |
| 11 | Superior Adjustment | 15 |

In the development of the questionnaire we relied, in part, on Engel's (1959) Q-sort and on our own Q-sort, which had been developed for another study (Marcus et al., 1966). The content of many of the items was also influenced by the following works: Garmezy, Clarke, and Stochner (1957); Coleman (1961); Erikson (1950); A. Freud (1946, 1958); Friedenberg (1960); Gardner (1959); Murray (1938); Peck (1958); Polka (1954); Raush and Sweet (1961); Rosengren (1961); Shoben (1949); and Silber et al. (1961). The items and scales were checked for clarity and meaningfulness in discussions with several teenagers. In the next stage, a pilot study was carried out with a sample of forty teenage boys (ten psychiatric patients and thirty high-school students). As a result of the preliminary testing, some items were rewritten, and others were replaced.

## Administration and Scoring of the OSIQ

The questionnaire has been prepared for group administration. The questionnaire form has been devised so that it combines a simplicity in responding for the subjects with the ease of computer scoring for the test administrators. Brief instructions and an example accompany the OSIQ.

The subjects are asked to read the front page of the booklet and provide the requested personal information. Alternately, the examiner may choose to read the instructions and examples aloud, or have the subjects read them and ask questions, if necessary.

There is no time limit; each subject is to proceed at his own pace. Approximately forty minutes are ordinarily required for completion. The majority of subjects tested thus far have reacted positively to the experience.

Since each subject should respond to the questions in terms of his own feelings, the examiner attempts to avoid further structuring or interpretation in his answers to specific questions about any item. Requests for the meanings of words occur only rarely. Questions about the purpose of the testing are answered straightforwardly.

The examiner should check each test after completion to see that all questions have been answered. The simple response format serves to reduce item skipping, but a double check is always wise. The subjects can change a response by erasing or crossing out a circle. The examiner can remind subjects during the testing to answer all items to further insure completeness.

Half of the items in each scale are written positively, so that accepting an item as describing oneself gives one a positive score. The other half of the items are written negatively. They are reversed automatically in scoring the test. Alternating positive and negative items insures that the adolescent will at least read the questions carefully. An adolescent may feel that one item is much more important than another and have no way to indicate that fact. In addition, a subject may feel constrained to give one of the limited number of responses available to some item, even though his actual inclination would be to give some other response not on the test or to give several responses all at once. We are aware that each adolescent tested had much more to say about himself than was elicited. If left to his own devices, the adolescent might well have responded in different ways, but by and large, we believe that the OSIQ elicits enough useful and phenomenologically meaningful data about adolescents' self-image to outweigh the disadvantages of this method.

The task presented to the subject is to indicate how well each item describes him or her. A verbal description for each of six alternatives is provided at the top of each page. The subject responds circling a number (1 through 6) that is printed next to each item. The six responses and their numerical values are:

1.  Describes me very well.
2.  Describes me well.
3.  Describes me fairly well.
4.  Does not quite describe me.
5.  Does not really describe me.
6.  Does not describe me at all.

The adolescent who states that a particular positive statement describes him very well, well, or even fairly well is telling us that he is well-adjusted to his world. Items are reflected by subtracting the circled value from 7; for example, 4 ("Does not quite describe me") for a negative item becomes a 3 after reflection $(7 - 4 = 3)$. Thus, the highest possible score on an item is 6, which connotes poor adjustment. The lowest possible score on an item is 1, which connotes superior adjustment. A subject's raw score for any scale is the sum of the circled values for the positive and reflected negative items divided by the number of items in the scale, so scale scores also range from 1, superior adjustment, to 6, poor adjustment.

## GUIDELINES FOR DELETING INVALID OSIQ PROTOCOLS

These guidelines reflect our judgment about the kind of protocol that is likely to be a product of careless responding. In developing these guidelines, we looked at empirical distributions and tried to pick out points of discontinuity, that is, points beyond which there seemed to be a group of responses not on a continuum with the bulk of responses. A questionnaire would be ignored in compiling group averages or group distributions if it contained:

1. Ten or more missing item responses;
2. Two or more missing responses on any ten-item scale (three or more missing responses on any fifteen-item or four or more on any twenty-item scale);
3. Eight or more identical responses in a row.

We also examined inconsistent pairs, that is, a series of seven pairs of statements logically opposed in terms of meaning in order to delete the records of the most inconsistent subjects. This criterion did not work, in that, for whatever reason, many subjects responded differently to one item of a matched pair than they did to the other. It is possible that these subjects were affected differently by the negative and positive phasing of the respective items in the pairs. As a result, there was no particular distribution cutoff in inconsistency scores when inconsistencies in each group were relatively high (two or three of the seven pairs on the average).

Another relevant factor was the correlation of OSIQ scale scores within and across groups. The correlational finding was that the poorer the self-image, the more inconsistent the paired responses were. One possibility is that when an instrument tends to elicit generally positive scores when conscientiously taken, random responding results in poorer scores (Wylie, 1974). Even if this is true, though, the meaningfulness of specific item distributions as explained earlier (Ostrov, Offer, and Howard 1980) should eliminate most random responding, although some random responding cannot be ruled out. Another possibility is that people who are willing to say negative things about themselves are more willing to do so on negatively keyed than on positively keyed items, or vice versa. A third possibility is that people grow more (or less) defensive in the course of taking a self-image test, and that late items are responded to more (or less) favorably.

In the absence of information about these possibilities, and because of the prevalence of inconsistent responding, we decided to drop the statistic of the inconsistent pairs as a basis for screening. Had we used this criterion, many subjects with the poorest self-images would have been deleted. If such protocols reflect meaningful, if somewhat defensive test-taking behavior, then deleting them would be tantamount to losing important data.

## DESCRIPTION OF SCALES*

*1. Impulse Control.* This scale measures the extent to which the ego apparatus of the adolescent is strong enough to ward off the various pressures that exist in his internal and his external environments.

> Example 1.   Even under pressure, I manage to remain calm.
> Example 2.   I carry many grudges.

A low standard score suggests a person whose defensive structure is poorly organized. He has low frustration tolerance and often acts on impulse. A high standard score suggests a person with a well-developed ego apparatus that enables him to delay gratification.

*2. Emotional Tone.* This scale measures the degree of affective harmony within the psychic structure, the extent to which there is fluctuation in the emotions as opposed to feelings that remain relatively stable.

> Example 1.   I enjoy life.
> Example 2.   I am so very anxious.

A low standard score shows poor affective control or great emotional fluctuation. A high standard score shows that the individual has an ability to experience many affects satisfactorily.

*3. Body and Self-Image.* This scale indicates the extent to which the adolescent has adjusted to or feels awkward about his body.

---

* The analysis using raw scores was constructed in such a way as to show that the *lower* the score the healthier the self-image was. This method is no longer in use. In recent years we have used standard scoring techniques (see Appendix D). The 1970s normal sample served as our baseline. All other groups were compared to them. In the standard score technique, the higher the score, the healthier the self-image.

## Appendices

> Example 1.  I am proud of my body.
> Example 2.  I frequently feel ugly and unattractive.

A low standard score shows continuing confusion about body boundaries or awkwardness about body changes taking place in early adolescence (ages twelve to thirteen). A high standard score shows a well-structured self-concept with well-defined body boundaries.

4. *Social Relationships.* This scale concerns itself with object relationships and with friendship patterns.

> Example 1.  Being together with other people gives me a good feeling.
> Example 2.  I prefer being alone (to being with other kids my age).

A low standard score shows that the teenager has not developed good object relations, and that he sees himself as a lonely and isolated individual. A high standard score shows a well-developed capacity for empathy with others.

5. *Morals.* This scale measures the extent to which the conscience or superego has developed.

> Example 1.  I would not hurt someone just for the "heck of it."
> Example 2.  Telling the truth means nothing to me.

A low standard score demonstrates a poorly developed superego. A high standard score demonstrates a well-developed sense of duty, responsibility, and concern for others.

6. *Sexual Attitudes.* This scale concerns itself with the adolescent's feelings, attitudes, and behavior towards the opposite sex.

> Example 1.  Sexual experiences give me pleasure.
> Example 2.  The opposite sex finds me a bore.

A low standard score means a relatively conservative attitude towards sexuality. A high standard score means relative openness to sexuality.

7. *Family Relationships.* This scale is concerned with how the adolescent relates to his parents and the kind of relationships he has with his father and mother. It measures the emotional atmosphere in the home.

Example 1.   I can count on my parents most of the time.
Example 2.   I try to stay away from home most of the time.
Example 3.   When I grow up and have a family, it will be in at least
             a few ways similar to my own.

A low standard score shows a teenager who does not get along well with his parents, and indicates that there are major communication gaps between the adolescent and his parents. A high standard score shows an adolescent who communicates openly with his parents.

8. *Mastery of the External World.* This scale demonstrates how well an adolescent adapts to his immediate environment.

Example 1.   When I decide to do something, I do it.
Example 2.   I feel that I have no talent whatsoever.

A low standard score shows an inability to visualize the self in order to finish a task. A high standard score shows a well-functioning adolescent who is able to deal with a crisis.

9. *Vocational-Educational Goals.* One of the specific tasks of the adolescent is learning and planning for his vocational future. This scale measures how well he is faring in accomplishing this task.

Example 1.   A job well done gives me pleasure.
Example 2.   Only stupid people work.

A low standard score represents a failure on the part of the teenager to work well within the school system and to make reasonable plans for the future. A high standard score indicates an adolescent who works effectively within the educational system and who makes reasonable plans for the future.

10. *Psychopathology.* This scale should identify any overt or severe psychopathology.

Example 1.   I often feel that I would rather die than go on living.
Example 2.   I am confused most of the time.
Example 3.   No one can harm me just by not liking me.

**141**

A low standard score will point to severe psychopathology on a clinical level. A high standard score would point to the relative lack of overt symptomatology.

11. *Superior Adjustment.* This scale measures how well the adolescent copes with himself, significant others, and his world. This scale could also be defined as a measure of ego strength or coping ability.

> Example 1.   Dealing with new intellectual subjects is a challenge for me.
>
> Example 2.   Our society is a competitive one, and I am not afraid of it.
>
> Example 3.   I do not rehearse how I might deal with a real coming event.

A low standard score indicates that the adolescent does not deal adequately with his environment. A high standard score indicates a well-functioning coping system.

## RELIABILITY AND VALIDITY OF THE OSIQ

The OSIQ avoids the problem of interrater agreement reliability by having, in effect, only one rater, the subject himself, and by using an *a priori* scoring scheme, which allows computer scoring of questionnaires. Internal reliability is measured by a statistical method called alpha (Cronbach, 1970), which, when applied to OSIQ data, shows that the scales and the total score have moderately high and acceptable internal reliabilities (Offer, Ostrov, and Howard, 1977). Good internal consistency also is shown by intergroup differences at the item level. In general, inspection shows that inconsistent group differences among items in any one scale are rare.

Stability data were gathered in 1979 on a sample of normal teenagers from suburbs in the Chicago area. These data, obtained on two occasions six months apart, indicate that the scale scores are almost as stable as they are internally consistent. The stability coefficients for these data ranged from .48 to .84 for the scales, and was .73 for the total score. A similar study, using institutionalized juvenile delinquents, obtained comparable results (Vreeland, unpublished data). Evidence of the stability of the construct underlying these scores is also provided by a longitudinal study conducted by Offer in the 1960s (Offer, 1969, Offer and Offer, 1975) in which subjects chosen for their normality on the basis of their OSIQ scores proved to be consistently nondeviant and nonpsychopathological over an eight-year period.

As explained in Chapter 1, another aspect of any construct, including self-image, is the extent to which it is multidimensional. The OSIQ was designed to reflect eleven separate self-dimensions, each corresponding to an area of functioning thought to be important to adolescents on the basis of theoretical considerations. In theory, we would expect these dimensions to show a great deal of overlap because they are all variations on one theme, that is, the way adolescents think and feel about themselves. On the other hand, the overlap between any two should not be great if they are, in fact, to be considered separate dimensions. In practice, overlap between most of the scales is quite high, especially in the light of the size of their internal reliabilities. Nevertheless, distinctions among clusters of these scales are sufficient to justify retaining their separate identities.

For all objective measuring devices, the most important consideration is validity. The OSIQ items were designed to take advantage of the adolescents' capacity to decenter from, and report objectively about, themselves. The assumption is that plain language can capture self-perceptions in a way that is meaningful to both observers and subjects. The use of the OSIQ has confirmed to us that this instrument does elicit straightforward communications from teenagers.

Three separate studies (Offer, 1969; Coche and Taylor, 1974; and Hjorth, 1980) have addressed the issue of the correlation of the OSIQ with tests such as the Bell Inventory, the Minnesota Multiphase Personality Inventory (MMPI), and the Tennessee self-image test, that is, have addressed the issue of its concurrent validity. The findings of these studies were that moderate to high correlations exist between the OSIQ and these other instruments. The Hjorth study contains two particularly noteworthy results. The first is that the Body and Self-Image scale of the OSIQ correlates more highly with the same scale on the Tennessee than it does with any other scale of that test. The other finding is that in an analogous way, the Family Relations scale of the OSIQ correlates highly with the analogous scale of the Tennessee.

The other study we shall consider is the longitudinal study of adolescent boys described in Offer (1969) and Offer and Offer (1975). The purpose of that study was to increase understanding of the development of normal adolescent boys. In 1962, subjects were selected from two suburban high schools on the basis of their having scored in the average range on at least nine of the eleven OSIQ scales. We drew subjects from the average range because of a belief that a person who does not see himself in an extreme way is more likely to be psychologically normal than someone who sees himself in unusually positive or negative ways. Eight years of follow-up research showed that the subjects selected functioned in psychologically normal ways in every area of their lives. The length and intensity of the study conducted was such that the investigators felt comfortable in concluding that positive adjustment did characterize these subjects' lives.

We feel that the OSIQ is capable of being used to select a group of adolescents who are characterized by a particular range of personality characteristics. Other data suggest that even finer distinctions can be made.

For example, looking within the group of normals in the longitudinal study, Offer and Offer (1975) found three different types of adaptation to adolescence. These typologies, although they all are within the normal range, differ in terms of healthy adjustment to adolescence. The OSIQ mean scores of persons who take each route differ significantly, and the ranking of OSIQ means followed exactly the theoretical rankings with regard to the degree of mental health and adjustment shown by subjects in each of these three groups. It follows, therefore, that the OSIQ not only can identify normals, but also can discriminate among psychologically meaningful subgroups within populations of normals.

Finally, the reader is urged to turn to the newly revised manual (Offer, Ostrov, and Howard, 1981B) for a detailed description of the current uses of the OSIQ.

# APPENDIX B

### Percent Endorsement of the Offer Self-Image Questionnaire for Adolescents*

ITEM NUMBERS are those used in the Offer Self-Image Questionnaire. Percentages have been rounded to the nearest whole number. Responses to each item are on a scale from 1 to 6. Responses of 1 (describes me very well), 2 (describes me well), or 3 (describes me fairly well) constitute an endorsement of the item. Responses of 4 (does not quite describe me), 5 (does not really describe me), or 6 (does not describe me at all) represent a failure to endorse that item.

---

* N = 212 young male, 276 young female, 373 older male, and 524 older female American teenagers tested in the late 1970s.

# Appendices

## TABLE B–1
### The Psychological Self
### I. Impulse Control: Percent Endorsement for Each Normal Sample

| | | Percent Endorsing in Each Group | | | |
|---|---|---|---|---|---|
| Item | | Young Male | Older Male | Young Female | Older Female |
| 1. | I carry many grudges. | 29 | 24 | 18 | 15 |
| 8. | I "lose my head" easily. | 40 | 33 | 32 | 33 |
| 17. | At times I have fits of crying and/or laughing that I seem unable to control. | 31 | 26 | 47 | 47 |
| 34. | I can take criticism without resentment. | 57 | 64 | 50 | 59 |
| 50. | I get violent if I don't get my way. | 22 | 17 | 14 | 16 |
| 59. | Even under pressure I manage to remain calm. | 72 | 79 | 64 | 66 |
| 69. | I keep an even temper most of the time. | 78 | 78 | 81 | 79 |
| 81. | I fear something constantly. | 23 | 23 | 31 | 25 |
| 123. | Usually I control myself. | 87 | 87 | 94 | 92 |

## TABLE B–2
### The Psychological Self
### II. Emotional Tone: Percent Endorsement for Each Normal Sample

| | | Percent Endorsing in Each Group | | | |
|---|---|---|---|---|---|
| Item | | Young Male | Older Male | Young Female | Older Female |
| 32. | Most of the time I am happy. | 83 | 85 | 85 | 88 |
| 44. | I feel relaxed under normal circumstances. | 93 | 90 | 88 | 93 |
| 66. | I feel so very lonely. | 16 | 15 | 24 | 22 |
| 68. | I enjoy life. | 91 | 90 | 87 | 92 |
| 100. | Even when I am sad I can enjoy a good joke. | 86 | 80 | 83 | 82 |
| 130. | I frequently feel sad. | 26 | 20 | 31 | 29 |
| 12. | I feel tense most of the time. | 27 | 21 | 24 | 26 |
| 23. | I feel inferior to most people I know. | 19 | 17 | 16 | 14 |
| 38. | My feelings are easily hurt. | 40 | 37 | 58 | 66 |
| 54. | I am so very anxious. | 55 | 53 | 53 | 51 |

146

TABLE B–3

*The Psychological Self*
*III. Body and Self-Image:*
*Percent Endorsement for Each Normal Sample*

| Item | | Percent Endorsing in Each Group | | | |
|------|------|------|------|------|------|
| | | Young Male | Older Male | Young Female | Older Female |
| 6. | The recent changes in my body have given me some satisfaction. | 76 | 75 | 61 | 62 |
| 27. | In the past year I have been very worried about my health. | 24 | 19 | 30 | 23 |
| 42. | The picture I have of myself in the future satisfies me. | 82 | 80 | 79 | 81 |
| 57. | I am proud of my body. | 77 | 80 | 57 | 51 |
| 72. | I seem to be forced to imitate the people I like. | 29 | 28 | 25 | 23 |
| 82. | Very often I think I am not at all the person I would like to be. | 47 | 44 | 46 | 46 |
| 90. | I frequently feel ugly and un-attractive. | 26 | 21 | 46 | 42 |
| 94. | When others look at me, they must think that I am poorly developed. | 20 | 15 | 20 | 13 |
| 99. | I feel strong and healthy. | 89 | 86 | 85 | 85 |

## TABLE B–4

*The Social Self*

*IV. Social Relationships: Percent Endorsement for Each Normal Sample*

| Item | | Percent Endorsing in Each Group | | | |
|------|---|------|------|------|------|
| | | Young Male | Older Male | Young Female | Older Female |
| 13. | I usually feel out of place at picnics and parties. | 25 | 22 | 24 | 19 |
| 52. | I think that other people just do not like me. | 21 | 16 | 23 | 16 |
| 65. | I do not mind being corrected since I can learn from it. | 79 | 82 | 77 | 81 |
| 62. | I find it extremely hard to make friends. | 17 | 15 | 13 | 13 |
| 75. | I prefer being alone than with other kids my age. | 24 | 21 | 23 | 18 |
| 86. | If others disapprove of me I get terribly upset. | 34 | 34 | 44 | 44 |
| 88. | Being together with other people gives me a good feeling. | 92 | 90 | 95 | 95 |
| 113. | I do not have a particularly difficult time in making friends. | 75 | 80 | 79 | 82 |
| 124. | I enjoy most parties I go to. | 85 | 84 | 86 | 85 |

## TABLE B–5

*The Social Self*
*V. Morals: Percent Endorsement for Each Normal Sample*

| Item | | Percent Endorsing in Each Group | | | |
|---|---|---|---|---|---|
| | | Young Male | Older Male | Young Female | Older Female |
| 5. | I would not hurt someone just for the "heck of it." | 78 | 79 | 87 | 89 |
| 30. | I would not stop at anything if I felt I was done wrong. | 39 | 37 | 24 | 20 |
| 40. | I blame others even when I know I was at fault. | 43 | 34 | 25 | 25 |
| 48. | Telling the truth means nothing to me. | 11 | 12 | 3 | 3 |
| 67. | I do not care how my actions affect others as long as I gain something. | 14 | 15 | 10 | 7 |
| 74. | For me good sportsmanship in school is as important as winning a game. | 71 | 69 | 75 | 75 |
| 83. | I like to help a friend whenever I can. | 93 | 92 | 96 | 99 |
| 92. | If you confide in others you ask for troubles. | 27 | 26 | 25 | 21 |
| 116. | Eye for an eye and tooth for a tooth does not apply for our society. | 44 | 37 | 40 | 38 |
| 120. | I would not like to be associated with those kids who "hit below the belt." | 65 | 65 | 64 | 68 |

## TABLE B–6
### *The Social Self*
### *IX. Vocational-Educational Goals:*
#### *Percent Endorsement for Each Normal Sample*

| Item | | Percent Endorsing in Each Group | | | |
|---|---|---|---|---|---|
| | | Young Male | Older Male | Young Female | Older Female |
| 14. | I feel that working is too much responsibility for me. | 7 | 6 | 7 | 6 |
| 20. | Only stupid people work. | 5 | 5 | 3 | 2 |
| 37. | I am sure that I will be proud about my future profession. | 88 | 85 | 86 | 84 |
| 46. | I would rather sit around and loaf than work. | 27 | 23 | 17 | 16 |
| 58. | At times, I think about what kind of work I will do in the future. | 92 | 92 | 93 | 95 |
| 63. | I would rather be supported for the rest of my life than work. | 16 | 16 | 8 | 11 |
| 70. | A job well done gives me pleasure. | 94 | 95 | 97 | 98 |
| 79. | I feel that there is plenty that I can learn from others. | 90 | 93 | 92 | 95 |
| 104. | At times I feel like a leader and feel that other kids can learn something from me. | 75 | 78 | 63 | 69 |
| 115. | School and studying mean very little to me. | 17 | 23 | 13 | 18 |

TABLE B–7

*The Sexual Self*

VI. Sexual Attitudes: Percent Endorsement for Each Normal Sample

| Item | | Percent Endorsing in Each Group | | | |
|---|---|---|---|---|---|
| | | Young Male | Older Male | Young Female | Older Female |
| 10. | The opposite sex finds me a bore. | 14 | 14 | 12 | 10 |
| 16. | It is very hard for a teenager to know how to handle sex in a right way. | 24 | 22 | 34 | 28 |
| | N = | (176)* | (299) | (205) | (420) |
| 28. | Dirty jokes are fun at times. | 84 | 82 | 73 | 73 |
| | N = | (177) | (299) | (206) | (420) |
| 77. | I think girls/boys find me attractive. | 64 | 73 | 55 | 65 |
| 80. | I do not attend sexy shows. | 38 | 41 | 57 | 58 |
| | N = | (175) | (296) | (206) | (421) |
| 91. | Sexually I am way behind. | 18 | 21 | 23 | 20 |
| | N = | (174) | (299) | (203) | (416) |
| 97. | Thinking or talking about sex frightens me. | 10 | 8 | 10 | 8 |
| | N = | (177) | (298) | (207) | (420) |
| 117. | Sexual experiences give me pleasure. | 86 | 87 | 60 | 76 |
| | N = | (170) | (296) | (203) | (410) |
| 119. | Having a girl/boy friend is important to me. | 77 | 72 | 72 | 75 |
| 122. | I often think about sex. | 80 | 77 | 54 | 60 |
| | N = | (173) | (296) | (207) | (416) |

* In some samples, subjects did not take the Sexual Attitudes scale; therefore, this scale has fewer subjects than the other ten scales do. This is also true for Item 31, Scale X.

TABLE B–8

*The Family Self*
*VII. Family Relationships:*
*Percent Endorsement for Each Normal Sample*

| Item | | Percent Endorsing in Each Group | | | |
|------|--|-----------|-----------|-----------|-----------|
| | | Young Male | Older Male | Young Female | Older Female |
| 4. | I think that I will be a source of pride to my parents in the future. | 84 | 81 | 79 | 79 |
| 9. | My parents are almost always on the side of someone else, e.g., my brother or sister. | 37 | 31 | 31 | 28 |
| 15. | My parents will be disappointed with me in the future. | 6 | 6 | 6 | 8 |
| 21. | Very often I feel that my father is no good. | 16 | 17 | 18 | 16 |
| 24. | Understanding my parents is beyond me. | 18 | 17 | 21 | 18 |
| 26. | I can count on my parents most of the time. | 78 | 76 | 74 | 77 |
| 51. | Most of the time, my parents get along with each other. | 79 | 74 | 75 | 73 |
| 55. | When my parents are strict, I feel that they are right even if I get angry. | 54 | 54 | 58 | 58 |
| 60. | When I grow up and have a family, it will be in at least a few ways similar to my own. | 79 | 74 | 77 | 75 |
| 64. | I feel that I have a part in making family decisions. | 71 | 72 | 70 | 73 |
| 71. | My parents are usually patient with me. | 84 | 79 | 80 | 76 |
| 73. | Very often parents don't understand a person because they had an unhappy childhood. | 31 | 27 | 31 | 31 |
| 85. | Usually I feel that I am a bother at home. | 25 | 21 | 26 | 22 |
| 87. | I like one parent much better than the other. | 26 | 23 | 29 | 33 |
| 95. | My parents are ashamed of me. | 8 | 7 | 5 | 7 |
| 102. | I try to stay away from home most of the time. | 24 | 29 | 30 | 29 |
| 106. | I have been carrying a grudge against my parents for years. | 8 | 11 | 11 | 11 |
| 112. | Most of the time my parents are satisfied with me. | 87 | 86 | 89 | 85 |
| 118. | Very often I feel that my mother is no good. | 11 | 12 | 12 | 10 |

## TABLE B–9
*The Coping Self*
*VIII. Mastery of the External World:*
*Percent Endorsement for Each Normal Sample*

| | | Percent Endorsing in Each Group | | | |
|---|---|---|---|---|---|
| Item | | Young Male | Older Male | Young Female | Older Female |
| 3. | Most of the time I think the world is an exciting place to live in. | 69 | 77 | 77 | 79 |
| 19. | If I put my mind to it, I can learn almost anything. | 88 | 87 | 87 | 82 |
| 35. | My work, in general, is at least as good as the work of the guy next to me. | 75 | 77 | 78 | 79 |
| 41. | When I want something, I just sit around wishing I could have it. | 29 | 27 | 24 | 20 |
| 76. | When I decide to do something, I do it. | 83 | 83 | 86 | 85 |
| 103. | I find life an endless series of problems without solutions in sight. | 21 | 21 | 19 | 16 |
| 105. | I feel that I am able to make decisions. | 87 | 89 | 92 | 90 |
| 109. | I feel that I have no talent whatsoever. | 7 | 9 | 12 | 13 |
| 128. | I am fearful of growing up. | 18 | 21 | 21 | 29 |
| 129. | I repeat things continuously to be sure that I am right. | 49 | 44 | 42 | 38 |

TABLE B–10

*The Coping Self*

*X. Psychopathology:*

*Percent Endorsement for Each Normal Sample*

| Item | | Percent Endorsing in Each Group | | | |
|---|---|---|---|---|---|
| | | Young Male | Older Male | Young Female | Older Female |
| 2. | I am afraid that someone is going to make fun of me. | 25 | 18 | 25 | 22 |
| 22. | I am confused most of the time. | 12 | 15 | 20 | 20 |
| 29. | I often blame myself even when I'm not really at fault. | 33 | 39 | 45 | 43 |
| 31. | The size of my sex organs is normal. | 90 | 91 | 96 | 96 |
| | N = | (172) | (295) | (201) | (416) |
| 36. | Sometimes I feel so ashamed of myself that I just want to hide in a corner and cry. | 18 | 15 | 38 | 33 |
| 45. | I feel empty emotionally most of the time. | 22 | 21 | 23 | 14 |
| 61. | I often feel that I would rather die than go on living. | 16 | 16 | 26 | 20 |
| 78. | Other people are not after me to take advantage of me. | 64 | 62 | 64 | 69 |
| 93. | Even though I am continuously on the go, I seem unable to get things done. | 33 | 37 | 37 | 36 |
| 96. | I believe I can tell the real from the fantastic. | 84 | 81 | 79 | 84 |
| 108. | When I enter a new room I have a strange and funny feeling. | 37 | 31 | 36 | 30 |
| 111. | When I am with people I am bothered by hearing strange noises. | 16 | 13 | 14 | 12 |
| 126. | I do not have any fears which I cannot understand. | 74 | 75 | 67 | 67 |
| 127. | No one can harm me just by not liking me. | 74 | 71 | 67 | 62 |

## TABLE B–11
*The Coping Self*
*XI. Superior Adjustment:*
*Percent Endorsement for Each Normal Sample*

| Item | | Percent Endorsing in Each Group | | | |
|---|---|---|---|---|---|
| | | Young Male | Older Male | Young Female | Older Female |
| 11. | If I would be separated from all people I know, I feel that I would not be able to make a go of it. | 34 | 24 | 41 | 34 |
| 25. | I do not like to put things in order and make sense of them. | 10 | 11 | 10 | 9 |
| 39. | When a tragedy occurs to one of my friends, I feel sad too. | 80 | 83 | 92 | 97 |
| 43. | I am a superior student in school. | 51 | 48 | 47 | 45 |
| 49. | Our society is a competitive one, and I am not afraid of it. | 73 | 76 | 64 | 57 |
| 53. | I find it very difficult to establish new friendships. | 28 | 25 | 27 | 20 |
| 56. | Working closely with another fellow never gives me pleasure. | 32 | 34 | 29 | 21 |
| 84. | If I know that I will have to face a new situation, I will try in advance to find out as much as possible about it. | 85 | 77 | 84 | 85 |
| 89. | Whenever I fail in something I try to find out what I can do in order to avoid another failure. | 87 | 84 | 89 | 87 |
| 107. | I am certain that I will not be able to assume responsibilities for myself in the future. | 11 | 15 | 9 | 7 |
| 110. | I do not rehearse how I might deal with a real coming event. | 43 | 37 | 41 | 30 |
| 114. | I do not enjoy solving difficult problems. | 41 | 33 | 45 | 43 |
| 121. | Worrying a little about one's future helps to make it work out better. | 74 | 72 | 69 | 71 |
| 125. | Dealing with new intellectual subjects is a challenge for me. | 77 | 78 | 78 | 78 |

# APPENDIX C

The Offer Self-Image Questionnaire
Scale Scores, Means, and
Standard Deviations

TWO-WAY ANALYSES of variance were performed on the various cell means using the Social Sciences Computer Program. Scores are raw scale scores, not the standard scores used subsequently in these appendices (see Appendix D, for example) and throughout this book. Raw scale scores are formed by adding responses given to items in a scale and dividing by the number of items in the scale. Before adding, item responses are reversed when necessary so that all items are keyed in the same direction. Thus, a response of 2 on the 1 to 6 scale for a positively worded item such as Item 34, Scale 1 ("I can take criticism without resentment") is not reversed. At the same time, a response to a negatively keyed item such as Item 1, Scale 1 ("I carry many grudges") is reversed so that a 5 becomes a 2. As a result of these procedures, good adjustment is indicated by lower rather than higher scores. Also, as a result of these procedures, the raw scale score shows the average item response after the appropriate reversing. As an example, a score of 2 on Scale 1 implies that if all items were positively worded, the average response would have been 2, "Describes me well," on the 1 to 6 scale.

Standard scores were not used in this table because as an artifact of the standard scoring procedure, all 1970s normal groups have average standard scores of 50 and standard deviations of 15 on all scales. See Appendix D for details of this scoring procedure.

TABLE C–1

*OSIQ Scale Score Means and Standard Deviations for Young Male, Young Female, Older Male, and Older Female Normal American Adolescents* *

| Scale　　　　　　　　N = | Young Male 212 | Older Male 373 | Young Female 276 | Older Female 524 |
|---|---|---|---|---|
| **Psychological Self** | | | | |
| 1. Impulse Control | 2.78 | 2.69 | 2.81 | 2.77 |
| | .78 | .72 | .68 | .74 |
| 2. Emotional Control | 2.53[1] | 2.53[1] | 2.69[1] | 2.67 |
| | .72 | .70 | .80 | .73 |
| 3. Body and Self-Image | 2.61[1] | 2.58[1] | 2.91[1] | 2.80[1] |
| | .71 | .68 | .68 | .71 |
| **Social Self** | | | | |
| 4. Social Relationships | 2.49 | 2.46 | 2.48 | 2.39 |
| | .71 | .72 | .73 | .67 |
| 5. Morals | 2.74[1] | 2.72[1] | 2.47[1] | 2.38[1] |
| | .58 | .63 | .52 | .54 |
| 9. Vocational and Educational Goals | 2.08[1] | 2.10[1] | 2.08[1] | 1.98[1] |
| | .60 | .65 | .54 | .60 |
| **Sexual Self** | | | | |
| 6. Sexual Attitudes　　N = 176, 298, 206, 418 | 2.46[1] | 2.51[1,2] | 2.95[1,2] | 2.76[1,2] |
| | .69 | .61 | .66 | .65 |
| **Familial Self** | | | | |
| 7. Family Relationships | 2.42 | 2.45 | 2.45 | 2.43 |
| | .69 | .73 | .76 | .85 |
| **Coping Self** | | | | |
| 8. Mastery of External World | 2.48 | 2.47 | 2.51 | 2.49 |
| | .61 | .64 | .58 | .62 |
| 10. Psychopathology | 2.52[1,2] | 2.56[1,2] | 2.76[1,2] | 2.63[1,2] |
| | .65 | .60 | .66 | .66 |
| 11. Superior Adjustment | 2.70 | 2.67[3] | 2.72[3] | 2.62[3] |
| | .53 | .57 | .49 | .54 |
| Total Score | 2.54 | 2.52 | 2.59 | 2.52 |
| | .46 | .50 | .44 | .48 |

\* N = 1385 on all scales with the exception of the Sexual Self Scale.
[1] Sex contrast significant at p < .05 level
[2] Age by sex contrast significant at p < .05 level
[3] Age contrast significant at p < .05 level
(All other contrasts are not significant.)

# APPENDIX D

A Comparison of the Offer Self-Image
Questionnaire Standard Scores Across Eight
Different Populations

TABLE D–1

*A Comparison of OSIQ Standard Scores Across Eight Populations[1,2,3]*

| Scale | 1960s Normal | Australian[4,5,6] | Israeli[5,6] | Irish[5,6] |
|---|---|---|---|---|
| Psychological Self | *58.42 | *54.37 | 49.74 | *52.93 |
| 1. Impulse Control | (13.45) | (17.00) | (13.85) | (15.45) |
|  | *54.31 | *52.59 | 48.68 | 51.81 |
| 2. Emotional Tone | (14.53) | (15.93) | (14.46) | (16.18) |
|  | *55.97 | 48.99 | 50.33 | 50.70 |
| 3. Body and Self-Image | (14.10) | (16.08) | (14.09) | (15.33) |
| Social Self | *54.96 | *51.42 | 49.93 | 51.85 |
| 4. Social Relationships | (14.45) | (16.60) | (14.11) | (15.64) |
|  | *59.02 | *54.09 | 48.87 | 49.93 |
| 5. Morals | (15.92) | (18.28) | (13.96) | (16.39) |
|  | *52.97 | *51.60 | *46.82 | 49.27 |
| 9. Vocational and Educational Goals | (15.44) | (15.90) | (13.00) | (14.80) |
| Sexual Self | 50.45 | 48.65 | 47.79 | 50.70 |
| 6. Sexual Attitudes | (14.10) | (17.98) | (13.91) | (16.88) |
| Familial Self | *53.00 | 50.53 | 50.51 | 51.95 |
| 7. Family Relationships | (14.46) | (16.81) | (11.59) | (14.57) |
| Coping Self | *54.59 | 49.44 | 51.16 | *46.34 |
| 8. Mastery of the External World | (14.73) | (16.14) | (12.01) | (15.72) |
|  | *56.55 | 50.63 | 51.98 | 49.72 |
| 10. Psychopathology | (14.27) | (15.41) | (14.52) | (14.66) |
|  | *57.99 | 50.18 | *53.38 | 48.87 |
| 11. Superior Adjustment | (15.03) | (16.68) | (13.48) | (15.12) |
| Total Score | *58.00 | *52.03 | 50.11 | 50.72 |
|  | (14.78) | (16.96) | (13.18) | (14.25) |

# TABLE D-1 *(Continued)*

| Scale | Irish, Disturbed[6] | American, Disturbed[6] | American, Delinquent[6] | American, Physically Ill[6] |
|---|---|---|---|---|
| Psychological Self | *44.38 | 52.09 | 48.27 | 50.91 |
| 1. Impulse Control | (17.54) | (19.30) | (16.34) | (14.13) |
| | *41.90 | *42.94 | *44.51 | *46.56 |
| 2. Emotional Tone | (24.06) | (20.56) | (17.12) | (15.69) |
| | 45.74 | *46.58 | 48.90 | *46.58 |
| 3. Body and Self-Image | (21.60) | (18.13) | (15.44) | (15.92) |
| Social Self | *44.71 | 46.57 | 48.16 | 48.18 |
| 4. Social Relationships | (20.07) | (20.14) | (17.01) | (18.94) |
| | 49.38 | *53.36 | *46.65 | 50.61 |
| 5. Morals | (19.14) | (15.51) | (17.46) | (15.96) |
| | *45.56 | 46.99 | *47.06 | 49.00 |
| 9. Vocational and Educational Goals | (15.91) | (18.68) | (17.10) | (16.46) |
| Sexual Self | *38.27 | 48.18 | 51.66 | *41.69 |
| 6. Sexual Attitudes | (18.94) | (18.19) | (16.44) | (17.47) |
| Familial Self | *45.19 | *42.25 | *39.61 | 47.10 |
| 7. Family Relationships | (16.62) | (19.03) | (17.38) | (15.96) |
| Coping Self | *41.55 | *44.57 | *47.13 | 47.99 |
| 8. Mastery of the External World | (18.97) | (20.51) | (16.55) | (16.85) |
| | *44.98 | 48.44 | *44.96 | 47.98 |
| 10. Psychopathology | (18.69) | (19.20) | (16.83) | (17.06) |
| | *41.66 | 47.79 | *46.60 | 49.57 |
| 11. Superior Adjustment | (18.65) | (18.76) | (17.59) | (15.73) |
| Total Score | *42.57 | *45.85 | *44.43 | 47.67 |
| | (18.97) | (19.92) | (16.53) | (15.97) |

1.   The scores for each group are means. Standard deviations are in parentheses below means scores.

2.   Subjects were selected in each group first by locating the age by sex cell (young male, young female, older male, older female) with the fewest subjects. Then a number of subjects equal to the number of subjects in that cell were drawn randomly from each of the other age by sex cells; the subjects thus chosen were pooled into one 1960s normal or Australian group, and so on. As a result of this procedure, the subjects in each group are as likely to be younger (12–15 years old) as older (16–19 years old) and as likely to be male as female. Standard scores were generated by using age by sex-appropriate 1970 normal reference group means and standard deviations. Appropriate reference group means were subtracted from each subject's scores, and that result was divided by the reference group standard deviation. The quotient was multiplied by 15 and 50 was added to that product. As a result, a score of 50 signifies a score equal to the appropriate normal reference group mean. A score lower or higher than 50 signifies, respectively, poorer or better adjustment than that of normals on a particular scale or on the total score. The standard deviations can be interpreted by comparing them to 15. A number larger than 15 implies a group standard deviation larger than is found in the normal reference group; a number smaller than 15 implies a group standard deviation smaller than is found in the normal reference group.

3.   Group means that are significantly different at the .05 level (two-tailed test) from corresponding 1970s normal reference group means are marked with an asterisk.

4.   Only young males and females were used for this group because no scores for older subjects were available.

5.   Results are not comparable to those presented in Offer, Ostrov, and Howard (1977) because those cross-cultural comparisons were made using 1960s American data.

6.   Australian subjects were tested in the 1960s. Other groups were tested in the 1970s.

# APPENDIX E

Percent Endorsement of the
Offer Self-Image Questionnaire
for Eight
Teenage Populations

THE PERCENT endorsements were calculated separately for younger males, older males, younger females, and older females for each population. The percentages reported in this table are averages across the four age-by-sex groups for each item and for each population. Australian subjects were tested in the 1960s. Irish, Israeli, American delinquent, American disturbed, and American physically ill subjects were tested in the 1970s.

## TABLE E-1

Percent Endorsement by Eight Teenage Populations of OSIQ Items Constituting the Psychological Self:
I. Impulse Control

| Item | | Normal American 1970s | Normal American 1960s | Australian | Irish | Israeli | Delinquent | Disturbed | Physically Ill |
|---|---|---|---|---|---|---|---|---|---|
| 1. | I carry many grudges. | 21 | 19 | 15 | 17 | 41 | 28 | 22 | 32 |
| 8. | I "lose my head" easily. | 35 | 21 | 29 | 32 | 19 | 39 | 32 | 30 |
| 17. | At times I have fits of crying and/or laughing that I seem unable to control. | 38 | 23 | 33 | 36 | 27 | 39 | 30 | 39 |
| 34. | I can take criticism without resentment. | 57 | 70 | 61 | 68 | 60 | 57 | 61 | 58 |
| 50. | I get violent if I don't get my way. | 17 | 5 | 12 | 13 | 15 | 20 | 17 | 15 |
| 59. | Even under pressure I manage to remain calm. | 70 | 75 | 64 | 67 | 56 | 69 | 68 | 64 |
| 69. | I keep an even temper most of the time. | 79 | 85 | 76 | 81 | 69 | 75 | 77 | 80 |
| 81. | I fear something constantly. | 25 | 17 | 25 | 40 | 26 | 37 | 30 | 25 |
| 123. | Usually I control myself. | 90 | 93 | 85 | 87 | 89 | 84 | 83 | 89 |

# TABLE E-2

Percent Endorsement by Eight Teenage Populations of OSIQ Items Constituting the Psychological Self:
II. Emotional Tone

| Item | Normal American 1970s | Normal American 1960s | Australian | Irish | Israeli | Delinquent | Disturbed | Physically Ill |
|---|---|---|---|---|---|---|---|---|
| 12. I feel tense most of the time. | 25 | 21 | 23 | 24 | 16 | 41 | 33 | 27 |
| 23. I feel inferior to most people I know. | 17 | 11 | 21 | 23 | 11 | 24 | 28 | 24 |
| 32. Most of the time I am happy. | 85 | 84 | 89 | 87 | 69 | 75 | 64 | 81 |
| 38. My feelings are easily hurt. | 50 | 39 | 49 | 53 | 57 | 48 | 53 | 50 |
| 44. I feel relaxed under normal circumstances. | 91 | 81 | 89 | 90 | 80 | 79 | 79 | 82 |
| 54. I am so very anxious. | 53 | 43 | 41 | 41 | 9 | 51 | 46 | 53 |
| 66. I feel so very lonely. | 19 | 18 | 18 | 19 | 9 | 31 | 34 | 23 |
| 68. I enjoy life. | 90 | 93 | 88 | 90 | 77 | 82 | 74 | 83 |
| 100. Even when I am sad, I can enjoy a good joke. | 83 | 84 | 83 | 81 | 65 | 74 | 79 | 78 |
| 130. I frequently feel sad. | 27 | 19 | 31 | 35 | 33 | 37 | 39 | 28 |

## TABLE E-3

*Percent Endorsement by Eight Teenage Populations of OSIQ Items Constituting the Psychological Self: III. Body and Self-Image*

| Item | Normal American 1970s | Normal American 1960s | Australian | Irish | Israeli | Delinquent | Disturbed | Physically Ill |
|---|---|---|---|---|---|---|---|---|
| 6. The recent changes in my body have given me some satisfaction. | 69 | 81 | 64 | 69 | 71 | 67 | 61 | 59 |
| 27. In the past year I have been very worried about my health. | 24 | 14 | 19 | 23 | 23 | 38 | 29 | 41 |
| 42. The picture I have of myself in the future satisfies me. | 81 | 74 | 75 | 71 | 60 | 72 | 70 | 78 |
| 57. I am proud of my body. | 66 | 68 | 67 | 69 | 39 | 71 | 61 | 59 |
| 72. I seem to be forced to imitate the people I like. | 26 | 27 | 31 | 35 | 12 | 24 | 25 | 24 |
| 82. Very often I think I am not at all the person I would like to be. | 46 | 36 | 61 | 55 | 30 | 51 | 49 | 44 |
| 90. I frequently feel ugly and unattractive. | 34 | 31 | 50 | 39 | 26 | 28 | 36 | 43 |
| 94. When others look at me they must think that I am poorly developed. | 17 | 8 | 17 | 17 | 13 | 17 | 20 | 15 |
| 99. I feel strong and healthy. | 86 | 94 | 85 | 83 | 78 | 79 | 76 | 77 |

## TABLE E-4

Percent Endorsement by Eight Teenage Populations of OSIQ Items Constituting the Social Self: IV. Social Relationships

| Item | Normal American 1970s | Normal American 1960s | Australian | Irish | Israeli | Delinquent | Disturbed | Physically Ill |
|---|---|---|---|---|---|---|---|---|
| 13. I usually feel out of place at picnics and parties. | 23 | 13 | 29 | 22 | 19 | 27 | 31 | 33 |
| 52. I think that other people just do not like me. | 19 | 19 | 23 | 20 | 15 | 25 | 29 | 25 |
| 62. I find it extremely hard to make friends. | 80 | 87 | 85 | 83 | 77 | 82 | 80 | 81 |
| 65. I do not mind being corrected, since I can learn from it. | 15 | 10 | 19 | 19 | 17 | 21 | 26 | 20 |
| 75. I prefer being alone than with other kids my age. | 21 | 15 | 28 | 19 | 9 | 31 | 25 | 23 |
| 86. If others disapprove of me I get terribly upset. | 39 | 23 | 41 | 40 | 14 | 39 | 45 | 36 |
| 88. Being together with other people gives me a good feeling. | 93 | 91 | 90 | 87 | 58 | 87 | 87 | 89 |
| 113. I do not have a particularly difficult time in making friends. | 79 | 85 | 78 | 72 | 66 | 69 | 68 | 72 |
| 124. I enjoy most parties I go to. | 85 | 80 | 88 | 88 | 85 | 82 | 78 | 80 |

## TABLE E-5

Percent Endorsement by Eight Teenage Populations of OSIQ Items Constituting the Social Self:
V. Morals

| Item | Normal American 1970s | Normal American 1960s | Australian | Irish | Israeli | Delinquent | Disturbed | Physically Ill |
|---|---|---|---|---|---|---|---|---|
| 5. I would not hurt someone just for the "heck of it." | 83 | 82 | 73 | 79 | 83 | 72 | 82 | 78 |
| 30. I would not stop at anything if I was done wrong. | 30 | 25 | 25 | 31 | 43 | 37 | 30 | 31 |
| 40. I blame others even when I know I was at fault. | 32 | 21 | 27 | 30 | 25 | 29 | 31 | 26 |
| 48. Telling the truth means nothing to me. | 7 | 9 | 11 | 17 | 13 | 19 | 9 | 11 |
| 67. I do not care how my actions affect others as long as I gain something. | 11 | 10 | 17 | 13 | 15 | 23 | 14 | 12 |
| 74. For me, good sportsmanship in school is as important as winning a game. | 73 | 86 | 83 | 77 | 68 | 71 | 69 | 78 |
| 83. I like to help a friend when I can. | 95 | 96 | 96 | 97 | 93 | 92 | 93 | 94 |
| 92. If you confide in others you ask for troubles. | 25 | 13 | 23 | 26 | 40 | 33 | 29 | 22 |
| 116. Eye for an eye and tooth for a tooth does not apply to our society. | 40 | 67 | 41 | 49 | 45 | 47 | 57 | 41 |
| 120. I would not like to be associated with those kids who "hit below the belt." | 65 | 75 | 67 | 56 | 80 | 58 | 63 | 65 |

Percent Endorsement by Eight Teenage Populations of OSIQ Items Constituting the Social Self:
IX. Vocational-Educational Goals

| Item | Normal American 1970s | Normal American 1960s | Australian | Irish | Israeli | Delinquent | Disturbed | Physically Ill |
|---|---|---|---|---|---|---|---|---|
| 14. I feel that working is too much responsibility for me. | 7 | 6 | 7 | 13 | 28 | 13 | 14 | 12 |
| 20. Only stupid people work. | 4 | 3 | 3 | 4 | 5 | 7 | 4 | 5 |
| 37. I am sure that I will be proud about my future profession. | 86 | 87 | 87 | 74 | 71 | 77 | 75 | 88 |
| 46. I would rather sit around and loaf than work. | 21 | 13 | 15 | 13 | 15 | 19 | 24 | 30 |
| 58. At times I think about what kind of work I will do in the future. | 93 | 89 | 91 | 93 | 91 | 89 | 91 | 91 |
| 63. I would rather be supported for the rest of my life than work. | 13 | 9 | 11 | 14 | 4 | 13 | 15 | 13 |
| 70. A job well done gives me pleasure. | 96 | 97 | 97 | 97 | 96 | 93 | 95 | 93 |
| 79. I feel that there is plenty that I can learn from others. | 93 | 91 | 91 | 95 | 83 | 86 | 93 | 89 |
| 104. At times I feel like a leader and feel that other kids can learn something from me. | 71 | 72 | 45 | 49 | 55 | 69 | 69 | 71 |
| 115. School and studying mean very little to me. | 18 | 15 | 12 | 19 | 11 | 35 | 31 | 18 |

## TABLE E-7

### Percent Endorsement by Eight Teenage Populations of OSIQ Items Constituting the Sexual Self: VI. Sexual Attitudes

| Item | Normal American 1970s | Normal American 1960s | Australian | Irish | Israeli | Delinquent | Disturbed | Physically Ill |
|---|---|---|---|---|---|---|---|---|
| 10. The opposite sex finds me a bore. | 13 | 10 | 15 | 16 | 12 | 12 | 15 | 16 |
| 16. It is very hard for a teenager to know how to handle sex in a right way. | 27 | 21 | 39 | 40 | 38 | 27 | 29 | 34 |
| 28. Dirty jokes are fun at times. | 78 | 58 | 68 | 76 | 59 | 63 | 70 | 54 |
| 77. I think girls/boys find me attractive. | 64 | 79 | 51 | 62 | 44 | 72 | 59 | 56 |
| 80. I do not attend sexy shows. | 49 | 43 | 45 | 51 | 33 | 47 | 55 | 51 |
| 91. Sexually I am way behind. | 21 | 7 | 16 | 17 | 11 | 15 | 18 | 32 |
| 97. Thinking or talking about sex frightens me. | 9 | 10 | 7 | 9 | 9 | 12 | 14 | 14 |
| 117. Sexual experiences give me pleasure. | 77 | 67 | 52 | 71 | 63 | 74 | 73 | 60 |
| 119. Having a girl/boyfriend is important to me. | 74 | 65 | 69 | 73 | 75 | 71 | 73 | 66 |
| 122. I often think about sex. | 68 | 63 | 67 | 72 | 60 | 58 | 65 | 53 |

# TABLE E–8

Percent Endorsement by Eight Teenage Populations of OSIQ Items Constituting the Familial Self: VII. Family Relationships

| Item | Normal American 1970s | Normal American 1960s | Australian | Irish | Israeli | Delinquent | Disturbed | Physically Ill |
|---|---|---|---|---|---|---|---|---|
| 4. I think that I will be a source of pride to my parents in the future. | 81 | 85 | 75 | 69 | 84 | 71 | 66 | 86 |
| 9. My parents are almost always on the side of someone else, eg. my brother or sister. | 32 | 14 | 39 | 27 | 20 | 35 | 31 | 37 |
| 15. My parents will be disappointed with me in the future. | 7 | 17 | 11 | 12 | 8 | 17 | 20 | 12 |
| 21. Very often I feel that my father is no good. | 17 | 15 | 17 | 15 | 17 | 25 | 24 | 22 |
| 24. Understanding my parents is beyond me. | 19 | 15 | 23 | 19 | 17 | 33 | 26 | 25 |
| 26. I can count on my parents most of the time. | 76 | 82 | 74 | 79 | 68 | 65 | 67 | 74 |
| 51. Most of the time my parents get along with each other. | 75 | 79 | 79 | 82 | 73 | 62 | 65 | 70 |
| 55. When my parents are strict, I feel that they are right even if I get angry. | 56 | 65 | 69 | 63 | 64 | 58 | 51 | 63 |

## TABLE E-8 (Continued)

| Item | Normal American 1970s | Normal American 1960s | Australian | Irish | Israeli | Delinquent | Disturbed | Physically Ill |
|---|---|---|---|---|---|---|---|---|
| 60. When I grow up and have a family, it will be in at least a few ways similar to my own. | 76 | 71 | 69 | 73 | 76 | 49 | 59 | 62 |
| 64. I feel that I have a part in making family decisions. | 71 | 78 | 63 | 69 | 24 | 67 | 65 | 66 |
| 71. My parents are usually patient with me. | 80 | 87 | 81 | 86 | 85 | 65 | 69 | 79 |
| 73. Very often parents don't understand a person because they had an unhappy childhood | 30 | 23 | 35 | 35 | 27 | 41 | 32 | 28 |
| 85. Usually, I feel that I am a bother at home. | 23 | 19 | 31 | 28 | 11 | 43 | 42 | 36 |
| 87. I like one parent much better than the other. | 28 | 18 | 28 | 22 | 21 | 42 | 33 | 30 |
| 95. My parents are ashamed of me. | 7 | 4 | 5 | 7 | 3 | 23 | 23 | 12 |
| 102. I try to stay away from home most of the time. | 28 | 25 | 23 | 23 | 30 | 49 | 46 | 29 |
| 106. I have been carrying a grudge against my parents for years. | 10 | 6 | 11 | 6 | 9 | 26 | 19 | 13 |
| 112. Most of the time, my parents are satisfied with me. | 87 | 84 | 87 | 83 | 87 | 59 | 65 | 81 |
| 118. Very often I feel that my mother is no good. | 11 | 8 | 11 | 9 | 7 | 19 | 18 | 13 |

## TABLE E-9

Percent Endorsement by Eight Teenage Populations of OSIQ Items Constituting the Coping Self: VIII. Mastery of the External World

| Item | Normal American 1970s | Normal American 1960s | Australian | Irish | Israeli | Delinquent | Disturbed | Physically Ill |
|---|---|---|---|---|---|---|---|---|
| 3. Most of the time I think the world is an exciting place to live in. | 75 | 86 | 77 | 75 | 87 | 71 | 64 | 72 |
| 19. If I put my mind to it, I can learn almost anything. | 86 | 87 | 82 | 79 | 90 | 88 | 84 | 86 |
| 35. My work, in general, is at least as good as the work of the guy next to me. | 77 | 78 | 85 | 80 | 87 | 72 | 71 | 74 |
| 41. When I want something I just sit around wishing I could have it. | 25 | 15 | 31 | 37 | 23 | 34 | 29 | 32 |
| 76. When I decide to do something, I do it. | 84 | 84 | 81 | 77 | 82 | 81 | 74 | 80 |
| 103. I find life an endless series of problems without solutions in sight. | 19 | 28 | 21 | 22 | 17 | 31 | 30 | 19 |
| 105. I feel that I am able to make decisions. | 89 | 91 | 79 | 79 | 88 | 87 | 83 | 85 |
| 109. I feel that I have no talent whatsoever. | 10 | 9 | 19 | 17 | 11 | 15 | 15 | 19 |
| 128. I am fearful of growing up. | 22 | 15 | 13 | 21 | 17 | 23 | 29 | 18 |
| 129. I repeat things continuously to be sure that I am right. | 43 | 31 | 53 | 56 | 59 | 49 | 40 | 53 |

## TABLE E-10

Percent Endorsement by Eight Teenage Populations of OSIQ Items Constituting the Coping Self: X. Psychopathology

| Item | Normal American 1970s | Normal American 1960s | Australian | Irish | Israeli | Delinquent | Disturbed | Physically Ill |
|---|---|---|---|---|---|---|---|---|
| 2. I am afraid that someone is going to make fun of me. | 23 | 20 | 32 | 30 | 24 | 28 | 31 | 31 |
| 22. I am confused most of the time. | 17 | 11 | 16 | 23 | 12 | 35 | 27 | 25 |
| 29. I often blame myself even when I'm not really at fault. | 40 | 33 | 45 | 41 | 41 | 44 | 43 | 45 |
| 31. The size of my sex organs is normal. | 93 | 92 | 93 | 93 | 94 | 90 | 88 | 87 |
| 36. Sometimes I feel so ashamed of myself that I just want to hide in a corner and cry. | 26 | 20 | 29 | 26 | 19 | 37 | 33 | 32 |
| 45. I feel empty emotionally most of the time. | 20 | 9 | 22 | 23 | 20 | 31 | 24 | 28 |
| 61. I often feel that I would rather die than go on living. | 19 | 13 | 29 | 25 | 23 | 34 | 29 | 26 |
| 78. Other people are not after me to take advantage of me. | 65 | 79 | 57 | 59 | 73 | 58 | 67 | 67 |

## TABLE E-10 (Continued)

| Item | Normal American 1970s | Normal American 1960s | Australian | Irish | Israeli | Delinquent | Disturbed | Physically Ill |
|---|---|---|---|---|---|---|---|---|
| 93. Even though I am continuously on the go, I seem unable to get things done. | 36 | 27 | 41 | 41 | 23 | 46 | 39 | 36 |
| 96. I believe I can tell the real from the fantastic. | 82 | 88 | 71 | 71 | 89 | 81 | 81 | 79 |
| 108. When I enter a new room I have a strange and funny feeling. | 33 | 24 | 39 | 38 | 35 | 49 | 39 | 40 |
| 111. When I am with people I am bothered by hearing strange noises. | 14 | 12 | 11 | 14 | 12 | 14 | 11 | 17 |
| 126. I do not have many fears which I cannot understand. | 71 | 79 | 79 | 73 | 73 | 67 | 69 | 75 |
| 127. No one can harm me just by not liking me. | 69 | 71 | 75 | 69 | 51 | 70 | 66 | 71 |

## TABLE E-11

Percent Endorsement by Eight Teenage Populations of OSIQ Items Constituting the Coping Self: XI. Superior Adjustment

| Item | Normal American 1970s | Normal American 1960s | Australian | Irish | Israeli | Delinquent | Disturbed | Physically Ill |
|------|------|------|------|------|------|------|------|------|
| 11. If I would be separated from all people I know, I feel that I would not be able to make a go of it. | 33 | 24 | 49 | 47 | 35 | 42 | 40 | 43 |
| 25. I do not like to put things in order and make sense of them. | 10 | 10 | 15 | 17 | 11 | 19 | 13 | 14 |
| 39. When a tragedy occurs to one of my friends, I feel sad too. | 88 | 89 | 89 | 88 | 88 | 87 | 86 | 85 |
| 43. I am a superior student in school. | 48 | 55 | 32 | 28 | 46 | 35 | 37 | 43 |
| 49. Our society is a competitive one, and I am not afraid of it. | 67 | 77 | 75 | 64 | 51 | 63 | 59 | 70 |
| 53. I find it very difficult to establish new friendships. | 25 | 24 | 26 | 31 | 20 | 30 | 32 | 33 |
| 56. Working closely with another fellow never gives me pleasure. | 29 | 12 | 21 | 27 | 20 | 27 | 21 | 23 |
| 84. If I know that I will have to face a new situation, I will try in advance to find out as much as possible about it. | 83 | 88 | 86 | 90 | 87 | 81 | 65 | 80 |
| 89. Whenever I fail in something I try to find out what I can do in order to avoid another failure. | 87 | 87 | 86 | 87 | 88 | 81 | 82 | 89 |

TABLE E-11 (Continued)

| Item | Normal American 1970s | Normal American 1960s | Australian | Irish | Israeli | Delinquent | Disturbed | Physically Ill |
|---|---|---|---|---|---|---|---|---|
| 107. I am certain that I will not be able to assume responsibilities for myself in the future. | 11 | 14 | 15 | 14 | 7 | 17 | 15 | 12 |
| 110. I do not rehearse how I might deal with a real coming event. | 27 | 38 | 41 | 41 | 40 | 47 | 43 | 43 |
| 114. I do not enjoy solving difficult problems. | 41 | 26 | 45 | 44 | 21 | 42 | 43 | 42 |
| 121. Worrying a little about one's future helps to make it work out better. | 71 | 75 | 67 | 68 | 81 | 67 | 65 | 62 |
| 125. Dealing with new intellectual subjects is a challenge for me. | 78 | 85 | 79 | 77 | 80 | 71 | 73 | 73 |

# REFERENCES

Ackerman, N. W. 1958. *The Psychodynamics of Family Life.* New York: Basic Books, Inc.

Adelson, J., ed. 1980. *Handbook of Adolescent Development.* New York: J. Wiley & Sons, Inc.

Adelson, J., and Doehrman, M. J. 1980. The Psychodynamic View of Adolescence: A Critical Analysis. In Adelson, J., ed., *Handbook of Adolescent Development.* New York: John Wiley & Sons, Inc.

Aichhorn, A. 1948. *Wayward Youth.* New York: Viking Press (English translation, 1948).

Anthony, J. 1969. The Reaction of Adults to Adolescents and Their Behavior. In Caplan, G. and Lebovici, S., eds., *Adolescence.* New York: Basic Books, Inc.

Atkins, J. W. 1974. Delinquency as a Function of Self-Esteem. *Dissertation Abstracts International* 34: 4650.

Bardwick, J. M. 1971. *Psychology of Women: A Study of Bio-Cultural Concepts.* New York: Harper & Row.

Berman, S. M. 1976. Validation of Social Self-Esteem and an Experimental Index of Delinquent Behavior. *Perceptual and Motor Skills* 13: 848–50.

Bettelheim, B. 1965. The Problem of Generations. In Erikson, E. H., ed., *The Challenge of Youth.* New York: Doubleday Anchor Books.

Beyer, M. 1974. Psychosocial Problems of Adolescent Runaways. *Dissertation Abstracts International* 35: 2420–21.

Bills, R. E., Vance, E. L., and McLean, O. S. 1951. An Index of Adjustment and Values. *Journal of Consulting Psychology* 15: 257–61.

Block, J. 1971. *Lives through Time.* Berkeley, Calif.: Bancroft Books.

Blos, P. 1962. *On Adolescence: A Psychoanalytic Interpretation.* New York: The Free Press.

Blos, P. 1967. The Second Individuation Process of Adolescence. *Psychoanalytic Study of the Child* XXII: 162–87.

Bradburn, N. 1969. *The Structure of Psychological Well-Being.* Chicago: Aldine.

Brennan, T. G., and O'Loídeain, D. S. 1980. A Comparison of Normal and Disturbed Adolescent Offer Self-Image Questionnaire Responses in an Irish Cultural Setting. *Journal of Youth and Adolescence* 9: 11–18.

Campbell, A. 1980. *The Sense of Well-Being in America: Recent Patterns and Trends.* New York: McGraw-Hill Book Co.

Casper, R., Offer, D., and Ostrov, E. 1981. The Self-Image of Adolescents with Anorexia Nervosa. American Journal of Pediatrics. (In press)

Chodorkoff, B. 1954. Self-Perception, Perceptual Defense, and Adjustment. *Journal of Abnormal and Social Psychology* 49: 508–12.

# References

Clifford, E. 1971. Body Satisfaction in Adolescence. *Perceptual and Motor Skills* 33: 119–25.

Coche, E., and Taylor, S. 1974. Correlations between the Offer Self-Image Questionnaire for Adolescents and the Minnesota Multiphasic Personality Inventory in a Psychiatric Hospital Population. *Journal of Youth and Adolescence* 3: 145–52.

Cole, C. W., Oetting, E. R., and Hinkle, J. E. 1967. Non-Linearity of Self-Concept Discrepancy: The Value Dimension. *Psychological Reports* 21: 58–60.

Coleman, J. S. 1961. *The Adolescent Society*. New York: The Free Press.

Collier, B. N., Jr. 1969. Comparisons between Adolescents with and without Diabetes. *Personnel & Guidance Journal* 47: 679–84.

Conger, J. J. 1975. *Contemporary Issues in Adolescent Development*. New York: Harper & Row.

Conger, J. J., and Miller, W. C. 1966. *Personality, Social Class, and Delinquency*. New York: John Wiley & Sons, Inc.

Coopersmith, S. 1967. *The Antecedents of Self-Esteem*. San Francisco: W. H. Freeman.

Cox Commission Report, 1968. *Crisis at Columbia*. New York: Vintage Books.

Cronbach, L. J. 1970. *Essentials of Psychological Testing*, 3rd ed. New York: Harper & Row.

Davis, A. 1944. Socialization and Adolescent Personality. In *Adolescents, Forty-Third Yearbook*, Part I. Chicago: Chicago Society for the Study of Education.

Deitz, G. E. 1969. A Comparison of Delinquents with Nondelinquents on Self-Concept, Self-Acceptance, and Parental Identification. *Journal of Genetic Psychology* 115: 285–95.

Deutsch, H. 1967. *Selected Problems of Adolescence*. New York: International Universities Press, Inc.

*Diagnostic and Statistical Manual of Mental Disorders*. 1980. 3rd ed. Washington, D.C.: American Psychiatric Association.

Douvan, E., and Adelson, J. 1966. *The Adolescent Experience*. New York: John Wiley & Sons, Inc.

Eissler, K. R. 1960. The Efficient Soldier. In Muensterburger, W., and Axelrod, S., eds., *The Psychoanalytic Study of Society*. New York: International Universities Press, 91–4.

Eissler, K. R. 1958. Notes on Problems of Technique in the Psychoanalytic Treatment of Adolescents. Psychoanalytic Study of the Child XIII: 223–54.

Elkin, F., and Westley, W. A. 1955. The Myth of Adolescent Culture. *American Sociological Review* 23: 680–83.

Engel, M. 1959. The Stability of the Self-Concept in Adolescence. *Journal of Abnormal and Social Psychology* 58: 74–83.

Erikson, E. H. *Childhood and Society*. 1950. New York: W. W. Norton and Company, Inc.

Erikson, E. H. 1959. Identity and the Life Cycle. *Psychological Issues*. New York: International Universities Press, pp. 1–171.

Erikson, K. 1962. Notes on the Sociology of Deviance. *Social Problems* 9: 307–14.

Evans, N. L. 1977. An Analysis of Self Concept and Attitudes toward School Scores and Their Relationship to the Iowa Test of Basic Skills between Nonpsychotic, Institutionalized, Acting Out, Emotionally Disturbed, and Normal School-Aged Children. *Dissertation Abstracts International* 38: 1994.

Fenichel, O. 1945. *The Psychoanalytic Theory of Neurosis*. New York: W. W. Norton and Company, Inc.

Ferguson, L. W., Freedman, M., and Ferguson, E. P. 1977. Developmental Self-Concept and (Self-Reported) Drug Use. *Psychological Reports* 41: 531–41.

Feuer, L. 1965. *The Conflict of Generations.* New York: Basic Books, Inc.

Fitts, W. H. 1965. *Tennessee Self-Concept Scale: Manual.* Nashville, Tenn.: Counselor Recordings and Tests.

Fountain, G. 1961. "Adolescent into Adult: An Inquiry. *Journal of the American Psychoanalytic Association* 9: 417–33.

Frank, S. J. 1978. Just Imagine How I Feel: How to Improve Empathy through Training in Imagination. In Singer, J. L. and Pope, K. S., eds., *The Power of Human Imagination,* New York: Plenum Press.

Freud, A. 1946. *The Ego and the Mechanisms of Defense.* New York: International Universities Press.

Freud, A. 1958. Adolescence. *Psychoanalytic Study of the Child* XVI: 255–78.

Freud, S. 1905. Fragment of an Analysis of a Case of Hysteria. In *The Standard Edition of the Complete Psychological Works of Sigmund Freud,* vol. 7, pp. 3–124.

Freud, S. 1913. Totem and Taboo. In *The Standard Edition of the Complete Psychological Works of Sigmund Freud,* vol. 13, pp. 1–164.

Freud, S. 1926. Inhibitions, Symptoms, and Anxiety. In *The Standard Edition of the Complete Psychological Works of Sigmund Freud,* vol. 20, pp. 77–179.

Freud, S. 1933. New Introductory Lectures on Psychoanalysis. In *The Standard Edition of the Complete Psychological Works of Sigmund Freud,* vol. 22, pp. 3–184.

Friedenberg, E. Z. 1960. *The Vanishing Adolescent.* Boston: Beacon Press.

Garber, B. 1972. *Follow-Up Study of Hospitalized Adolescents.* New York: Brunner/Mazel.

Gardner, G. 1959. Psychiatric Problems of Adolescence. In Arietti, S., ed., *American Handbook of Psychiatry.* New York: Basic Books, Inc.

Garmezy, N., Clarke, A. R., and Stochner, C. 1957. Child-Rearing Attitudes of Mothers and Fathers as Reported by Schizophrenic and Normal Control Patients. Ph.D. dissertation, Duke University.

Gecas, V. 1970. Parent-Child Interaction and Adolescent Self-Evaluation. *Dissertation Abstracts International* 30: 3562–63.

Geleerd, E. R. 1961. Some Aspects of Ego Vicissitudes in Adolescence. *Journal of the American Psychoanalytic Association* 9: 394–405.

Gesell, A., Ilg, F., and Ames, L. 1956. *Youth: The Years from Ten to Sixteen.* New York: Harper & Row.

Gildston, P. 1967. Stutterers' Self-Acceptance and Perceived Parental Acceptance. *Journal of Abnormal Psychology* 72: 59–64.

Gitelson, M. 1954. The Analysis of the "Normal" Candidate. *International Journal of Psychoanalysis* 35: 174–83.

Glueck, E. T. 1959. Spotting Potential Delinquents: Can It Be Done? In Glueck, S., ed., *The Problem of Delinquency.* Boston: Houghton Mifflin Company.

Glueck, S., and Glueck, E. T. 1950. *Unraveling Juvenile Delinquency.* New York: The Commonwealth Fund.

Goethe, J. 1774. *The Sorrows of Young Werther.* New York: New York Book Company (English translation, 1898).

Goffman, E. 1959. *The Presentation of Self in Everyday Life.* Garden City, New York: Doubleday Anchor Books.

Gold, M. 1970. *Delinquent Behavior in an American City.* Belmont, Calif.: Brooks-Cole.

Gold, M., and Mann, D. 1972. Delinquency as a Defense. *American Journal of Orthopsychiatry* 42: 463–71.

Goldman, R. K., and Mendelsohn, G. A. 1969. Psychotherapeutic Change and Social Adjustment. *Journal of Abnormal Psychology* 74: 164–72.

# References

Gonzalez-Tamayo, E. 1974. Dogmatism, Self-Acceptance, and Acceptance of Others among Spanish and American Students. *Journal of Social Psychology* 94: 15–25.

Gottuso, J. B. 1974. An Interpersonal Approach to Female Adolescent Delinquency. *Dissertation Abstracts International* 34: 5191.

Gregory, R. D. 1977. Self-Concept Across Sex, Color, and Teacher-Estimated, Annual Family Income Level for Students in Grades Seven through Twelve. *Dissertation Abstracts International* 38: 1859.

Grinker, R. R. 1957. On Identification. *The International Journal of Psychoanalysis* 38: 1–12.

Grinker, R. R. Sr., Grinker, R. R. Jr., and Timberlake, J. 1962. A Study of "Mentally Healthy" Young Males (Homoclites). *AMA Archives of General Psychiatry* 6: 405–53.

Hall, G. S. 1904. *Adolescence: Its Psychology and Its Relation to Physiology, Anthropology, Sociology, Sex, Crime, Religion, and Education.* New York: D. Appleton & Company.

Hamburg, D. A., Coelho, G. V., and Adams, J. E. 1974. Coping and Adaptation. In Coelho, G. V., Hamburg, D. A., and Adams, J. E., eds., *Coping and Adaptation.* New York: Basic Books, Inc.

Harley, R. B. 1973. Race, Fatherlessness, and Vocational Development: An Exploration of Relationships Between Membership in Nuclear or Fatherless Families and Level of Occupational Aspiration and Expectation, Self-Esteem, Extrinsic Work Values, and Person-Orientation Among a Sample of Black and White Adolescent Boys. *Dissertation Abstracts International* 33: 6090–91.

Harris, M. 1974. *Cows, Pigs, Wars, and Witches: The Riddles of Culture.* New York: Random House, Inc.

Hartmann, H. 1950. Comments on the Psychoanalytic Theory of the Ego. *The Psychoanalytic Study of the Child* V: 74–96.

Hauser, S. T. 1976. The Content and Structure of Adolescent Self-Images. *AMA Archives of General Psychiatry* 33: 27–32.

Healey, G. W., and Deblassie, R. R. 1974. A Comparison of Negro, Anglo, and Spanish-American Adolescents' Self-Concept. *Adolescence* 9: 15–24.

Healy, W., and Bronner, A. F. 1936. *New Light on Delinquency and Its Treatment.* New Haven, Conn.: Yale University Press.

Helland, D. J. 1973. Sex-Role Correlates of Adolescent Self-Esteem. *Dissertation Abstracts International* 34: 2026–27.

Hjorth, C. 1980. The Self-Concept, Self-Image and Body Image of the Physically Abused Adolescent. Ph.D. dissertation, California Graduate Institute (Los Angeles).

Hjorth, C., and Ostrov, E. 1981. The Self-Image of Abused Adolescents. Unpublished.

Holinger, P. C. 1980. Violent Deaths as a Leading Cause of Mortality: An Epidemiological Study of Suicide, Homicide, and Accidents. *American Journal of Psychiatry* 137: 472–76.

Holinger, P. C., and Offer, D. 1981A. Perspectives on Suicide in Adolescence. In Simmons, R. G., ed., *Research in Community and Mental Health,* vol. II. Greenwich, Conn.: JAI Press, Inc.

Holinger, P. C., and Offer, D. 1981B. Adolescent Suicide and Population Change. Unpublished.

Hoyte, M. 1976. A Study of the Relationship between Parenting, the Self-Concept, and Level of Vocational Maturity of the Male Adolescent. *Dissertation Abstracts International* 36: 6474–75.

Hsu, F. L. K. 1961. Culture Patterns and Adolescent Behavior. *International Journal of Social Psychiatry* 7: 33–53.

Jacobson, E. 1961. Adolescent Moods and the Remodeling of Psychic Structures in Adolescence. *Psychoanalytic Study of the Child* XVI: 164–183.

Jacobson, E. 1964. *The Self and the Object World*. New York: International Universities Press, Inc.

James, W. 1892. *Psychology, Briefer Course*. New York: Henry Holt & Co.

Jensen, G. F. 1972. Delinquency and Adolescent Self-Conceptions. A Study of the Personal Relevance of Infraction. *Social Problems* 20: 84–103.

Josselyn, I. M. 1952. *The Adolescent and His World*. New York: Family Services Association of America.

Josselyn, I. M. 1967. The Adolescent Today. *Smith College Studies in Social Work* 38: 1–15.

Kaplan, A. 1964. *The Conduct of Inquiry: Methodology for Behavioral Science*. San Francisco, Calif.: Chandler Publishing Company.

Kelly, G. A. 1963. *A Theory of Personality: The Psychology of Personal Constructs*. New York: W. W. Norton and Company, Inc.

Kett, J. F. 1977. *Rites of Passage: Adolescence in America, 1790 to the Present*. New York: Basic Books, Inc.

Kiell, N. 1959. *The Adolescent through Fiction: A Psychological Approach*. New York: International University Press, Inc.

Kitsuse, J. I. 1962. Societal Reaction to Deviant Behavior. *Social Problems* 9: 249–56.

Kohlberg, L. 1966. A Cognitive Developmental Analysis of Children's Sex-Role Concepts and Attitudes. In Maccoby, E., ed., *The Development of Sex Differences*. Stanford, Calif.: Stanford University Press.

Kohlberg, L., and Gilligan, C. 1971. The Adolescent as Philosopher. *Daedalus* 100: 1051–86.

Kohut, H. 1971. *The Analysis of Self: A Systematic Approach to the Psychoanalytic Treatment of Narcissistic Personality Disorders, The Psychoanalytic Study of the Child, Monograph No. 4*. New York: International Universities Press, Inc.

Kohut, H. 1980. Summarizing Reflections. In Goldberg, A., ed., *Advances in Self-Psychology*. New York: International Universities Press, Inc.

Laitman, R. J. 1975. Family Relations as an Intervening Variable in the Relationship of Birth Order and Self-Esteem. *Dissertation Abstracts International* 36: 3051.

Larson, J. R. 1976. An International Self-Evaluation Study of Fifteen- and Sixteen-Year-Old Students. *Dissertation Abstracts International* 37: 2079.

Laufer, M. 1966. Object Loss and Mourning during Adolescence. *Psychoanalytic Study of the Child* XXI: 269–94.

Lecky, P. 1945. *Self-Consistency: A Theory of Personality*. New York: Island Press.

Long, B. H., Ziller, R. C., and Bankes, J. 1970. Self-Other Orientations of Institutionalized Behavior-Problem Adolescents. *Journal of Consulting and Clinical Psychology* 34: 43–47.

McCord, W., McCord, J., and Zola, I. K. 1959. *Origins of Crime*. New York: Columbia University Press.

McFern, A. R. 1974. A Self-Concept Study of Adolescents in Four Areas of Exceptionality. *Dissertation Abstracts International* 34: 4040–41.

Mannes, M. 1978. Television: The Splitting Image. In Ferrell, W. A., and Salems, N. A., eds., *Strategies in Prose*. New York: Holt, Rinehart & Winston.

Mannheim, K. 1952. The Problem of Generations. In Kecskemeti, P., ed., *Essays on the Sociology of Knowledge*. London: Oxford University Press, Inc.

Marcus, D., Offer, D., Blatt, S., and Gratch, G. 1966. A Clinical Approach to the Understanding of Normal and Pathological Adolescence. *AMA Archives of General Psychiatry* 15: 569–76.

# References

Marohn, R. C., Offer, D., and Ostrov, E. 1971. Juvenile Delinquents View Their Impulsivity. *American Journal of Psychiatry* 128: 418–23.

Masterson, J. F., Jr. 1967. *The Psychiatric Dilemma of Adolescence*. Boston: Little, Brown & Company.

Matteson, R. 1974. Adolescent Self-Esteem, Family Communication, and Marital Satisfaction. *Journal of Psychology* 86: 35–47.

Mead, G. H. 1934. *Mind, Self, and Society*. Chicago: University of Chicago Press.

Mead, M. 1970. *Culture and Commitment*. Garden City, N.Y.: Doubleday and Company.

Meissner, A. L., Thoreson, R. W., and Butler, A. J. 1967. Relation of Self-Concept to Impact and Obviousness of Disability Among Male and Female Adolescents. *Perceptual and Motor Skills* 24: 1099–1105.

Merton, R. K. 1957. *Social Theory and Social Structure*, rev. ed. Glencoe, Ill.: The Free Press.

Miller, W. 1958. Lower Class Culture as a Generating Milieu of Gang Delinquency. *Journal of Social Issues* 14: 5–19.

Monge, R. H. 1973. Developmental Trends in Factors of Adolescent Self-Concept. *Developmental Psychology* 8: 382–93.

Morris, N., and Hawkins, G. 1970. *The Honest Politician's Guide to Crime Control*. Chicago: The University of Chicago Press.

Murray, C. A., Thomson, D., and Israel, C. B. 1978. *UDIS: Deinstitutionalizing the Chronic Juvenile Offender*. Washington, D. C.: American Institutes for Research.

Murray, H. A. 1938. *Explorations in Personality*. New York: Oxford University Press.

Musa, K. E., and Roach, M. E. 1973. Adolescent Appearance and Self-Concept. *Adolescence* 8: 385–94.

Nesselroade, J. R., and Baltes, P. B. 1974. Adolescent Personality Development and Historical Change: 1970–1972. *Monographs of the Society for Research in Child Development* 39: 1–79.

Newman, B. M., and Newman, P. R. 1979. *An Introduction to the Psychology of Adolescence*. Homewood, Illinois: The Dorsey Press.

Norem-Hebeisen, A. A. 1975. Differentiated Aspects of the Self-Esteeming Process among Suburban Adolescents and Dysfunctional Youth. *Dissertation Abstracts International* 35: 5130.

Nye, F. I. 1958. *Family Relationships and Delinquent Behavior*. New York: John Wiley & Sons, Inc.

Offer, D. 1969. *The Psychological World of the Teen-ager: A Study of Normal Adolescent Boys*. New York: Basic Books, Inc.

Offer, D., and Howard, K. I. 1972. An Empirical Analysis of the Offer Self-Image Questionnaire for Adolescents. *AMA Archives of General Psychiatry* 27: 529–37.

Offer, D., Marohn, R. C., and Ostrov, E. 1979. *The Psychological World of the Juvenile Delinquent*. New York: Basic Books, Inc.

Offer, D., and Offer, J. B. 1975. *From Teenage to Young Manhood: A Psychological Study*. New York: Basic Books, Inc.

Offer, D., Ostrov, E., and Howard, K. I. 1977. *The Offer Self-Image Questionnaire for Adolescents: A Manual*. Chicago: Michael Reese Hospital.

Offer, D., Ostrov, E., and Howard, K. I. 1981A. The Mental Health Professional's Concept of the Normal Adolescent. *AMA Archives of General Psychiatry* 38: 2, 149–53.

Offer, D., Ostrov, E., and Howard, K. I. 1981B. *The Offer Self-Image Questionnaire for Adolescents: A Manual*, rev. Chicago: Michael Reese Hospital. (In press)

Offer, D., and Sabshin, M. 1963. The Psychiatrist and the Normal Adolescent. *AMA Archives of General Psychiatry* 9: 427–32.

Offer, D., and Sabshin, M. 1974. *Normality: Theoretical and Clinical Concepts of Mental Health*, rev. ed., New York: Basic Books, Inc.

Orlinsky, D., and Howard, K. I. 1975. *Varieties of Psychotherapeutic Experience: Multivariate Analyses of Patients' and Therapists' Reports*. New York: Teachers College Press.

Ostrov, E., and Offer, D. 1980. Loneliness and the Adolescent. In Hartog, J., Audy, J. R., and Cohen, Y. A., eds., *The Anatomy of Loneliness*. New York: International Universities Press, Inc.

Ostrov, E., Offer, D., and Howard, K. I. 1980. Values and Self-Conceptions Held by Normal and Delinquent Adolescent Males. Unpublished.

Parsons, T. 1964. Age and Sex in the Social Structure of the United States. In *Essays in Sociological Theory*, rev. ed. New York: The Free Press.

Parsons, T. 1965. Youth in the Context of American Society. In Erikson, E. H., ed., *The Challenge of Youth*. New York: Doubleday Anchor Books.

Pearson, G. H. J. 1958. *Adolescence and the Conflict of Generations, An Introduction to Some of the Psychoanalytic Contributions to the Understanding of Adolescence*. New York: W. W. Norton and Company, Inc.

Peck, R. F. 1958. Family Patterns Correlated with Adolescent Personality Structure. *Journal of Abnormal and Social Psychology* 57: 347–50.

Perlin, S., Polin, W., and Butler, R. N. 1958. The Experimental Subject: 1. The Psychiatric Evaluation and Selection of a Volunteer Population. *AMA Archives of Neurology and Psychiatry* 86: 65–70.

Piaget, J. 1968. *Six Psychological Studies*. New York: Vintage Books.

Piaget, J. 1972. *The Child and Reality*. New York: Grossman Publishers (English translation, 1973).

Polka, S. K. 1954. The Influence of Temporary Projected Goals of Present Behavior. Unpublished Ph.D. Thesis, University of Kansas.

Popper, K. 1959. *The Logic of Scientific Discovery*. New York: Basic Books, Inc.

Porteus, S. D. 1945. Q-Scores, Temperament, and Delinquency. *The Journal of Social Psychology* 21: 81–103.

Preston, C. E. 1967. Self-Perceptions among Adolescents. *Psychology in the Schools* 4: 254–56.

Rabichow, H. G., and Sklansky, M. D. 1980. *Effective Counseling of Adolescents*. Chicago: Follett Publishing Co.

Rathus, S. A., and Siegel, L. J. 1973. Delinquent Attitudes and Self-Esteem. *Adolescence* 8: 265–76.

Raush, H., and Sweet, B. 1961. The Pre-Adolescent Ego: Some Observations of Normal Children. *Psychiatry* 24: 122–32.

Reckless, W. C., Dinitz, S., and Murray, E. 1956. Self-Concept as an Insulator Against Delinquency. *American Sociological Review* 21: 744–46.

Rogers, C. R. 1951. *Client-Centered Therapy: Its Current Practice, Implications, and Theory*. Boston: Houghton Mifflin Company.

Rogers, C. R., and Dymond, R. F., eds. 1954. *Psychotherapy and Personality Change*. Chicago: University of Chicago Press.

Rosenberg, M. 1965. *Society and the Adolescent Self-Image*. Princeton, N.J.: Princeton University Press.

Rosenberg, M. 1979. *Conceiving the Self*. New York: Basic Books, Inc.

Rosengren, W. R. 1961. The Self in the Emotionally Disturbed. *American Journal of Sociology* 66: 113–27.

Rutter, M., Graham, P., Chadwick, D. F. D., and Yule, W. 1976. Adolescent

# References

Turmoil: Fact or Fiction. *Journal of Child Psychology and Psychiatry* 17: 35–56.

Schachtel, E. G. 1950. Some Notes on the Use of the Rorschach Test. In Glueck, S., and Glueck, E., eds., *Unraveling Juvenile Delinquency*. New York: The Commonwealth Fund.

Schachter, S., and Singer, J. E. 1962. Cognitive, Social, and Physiological Determinants of Emotional State. *Psychological Review* 69: 376–79.

Schafer, R. 1979. The Psychoanalyst's Empathy. Mimeographed. Chicago: Chicago Psychoanalytic Society.

Schoeppe, A., and Havighurst, R. J. 1952. A Validation of Development and Adjustment Hypotheses of Adolescence *Journal of Educational Psychology* 43: 339–53.

Shafiabady, A. 1975. The Relationship Between Self Esteem and Anxiety Among High School Students in Grades Nine through Twelve. *Dissertation Abstracts International* 35: 7663–64.

Shaw, C. R., and McKay, H. D. 1969. *Juvenile Delinquency and Urban Areas*. Chicago: University of Chicago Press.

Shoben, E. J. 1949. The Assessment of Parental Attitudes in Relation to Child Adjustment. *General Psychological Monographs* 39: 101–48.

Short, J. F., Jr., and Strodtbeck, F. L. 1965. *Group Process and Gang Delinquency*. Chicago: University of Chicago Press.

Silber, E., Hamburg, D. A., Coelho, G. R., Murphy, E. B., Rosenberg, M., and Pearlin, L. I. 1961. Adaptive Behavior in Competent Adolescents. *AMA Archives of General Psychiatry* 5: 359–65.

Simmons, R. G., and Rosenberg, F. 1975. Sex, Sex Roles, and Self-Image. *Journal of Youth and Adolescence* 4: 229–58.

Smith, M. B. 1950. The Phenomenological Approach in Personality Theory: Some Critical Remarks. *Journal of Abnormal and Social Psychology* 45: 516–22.

Smith, M. B. 1978. Perspectives on Selfhood. *American Psychologist* 33: 1053–63.

Snider, J. G., Snider, J. A., Jr., and Nichols, K. E. 1968. Active-Passive Social Attitudes toward Self and Ideal-Self in Children in Canada and the United States. *Journal of Social Psychology* 76: 135–36.

Srole, L., and Fischer, A. K. 1980. Perspective: The Midtown Manhattan Longitudinal Study vs. "The Mental Paradise Lost" Doctrine. *AMA Archives of General Psychiatry* 37: 209–226.

Stone, L. J., and Church, J. 1979. *Childhood and Adolescence: A Psychology of the Growing Person*, 4th ed. New York: Random House, Inc.

Sullivan, H. S. 1953. *The Interpersonal Theory of Psychiatry*. New York: W. W. Norton & Company, Inc.

Uniform Crime Reports U.S. Census Bureau Statistics, 1960–1976.

United States Department of Labor Statistics, 1960–1976.

Vaillant, G. E. 1977. *Adaptation to Life*. Boston: Little, Brown and Company.

Vaillant, G. E., and McArthur, C. C. 1972. Natural History of Male Psychological Health. I. The Adult Life Cycle from 18–50. *Seminars of Psychiatry* 4: 4–16.

Walpole, J. W. 1973. A Survey of Drug Use and an Examination of the Relationship of Self-Perceptions and Adjustment to Adolescent Drug Abuse. *Dissertation Abstracts International* 34: 2403.

Walster, E., Aronson, B., Abrahams, D. and Rottman, L. 1966. The Importance of Physical Attractiveness in Dating Behavior. *Journal of Personality and Social Psychology* 4: 508–16.

Weiner, I. B. 1970. *Psychological Disturbance in Adolescence*. New York: Wiley-Interscience.

Weisser, S. 1981. Letting Go: Sexual Passion in the Victorian Novel. Ph.D. dissertation, Columbia University.

Weissman, M. M., and Klerman, G. L. Epidemiology of Mental Disorders. *AMA Archives of General Psychiatry* 35, 705–12.

Whisnant, L., and Zegans, L., 1975. A Study of Attitudes toward Menarche in White Middle-Class American Adolescent Girls. *American Journal of Psychiatry* 132: 809–14.

Wiggins, R. G. 1973. Differences in Self-Perceptions in Ninth-Grade Boys and Girls. *Adolescence* 8: 491–96.

Wylie, R. 1974. *The Self-Concept: A Review of Methodological Considerations and Measuring Instruments*, vol. 1, rev. ed. Lincoln, Nebraska: University of Nebraska Press.

Wylie, R. C. 1979. *The Self-Concept: Theory and Research*, vol. 2, rev. ed. Lincoln, Nebraska: University of Nebraska Press.

Young, F. W. 1965. *Initiation Ceremonies: A Cross-Cultural Study of Status Dramatization*. New York: The Bobbs-Merrill Company, Inc.

# INDEX

# Index

self-system, 22

self theory, 11, 12

sensitivity, and generational differences, 57

separation, in adolescence, 24, 93–94

sex: and attitudes toward sexuality, 62, table 5–1(p. 62), 63; and coping self-image, 74, table 7–2(p. 75), 75; and emotion, 47, table 3–2(p. 48); psychological self, and effect of, 47, table 3–2(p. 48); significant analysis in OSIQ sample, 37, 38; and social self, 55–56, table 4–2(p. 55); *see also* sex-related differences

sex distribution, of test sample, 33

sex-related differences, 95–101, table C–1(p. 157); and coping self, table 7–1(p. 73), table 7–2(p. 75); tables B–9 to B–11(pp. 153–55); and cultural influence, 97; and economic opportunity, 98; and familial self, table 6–1(p. 66), table B–8(p. 152); and moral values, 55, table 4–2(p. 55); and normal adolescents, 95–101; and psychological self, table 3–1(p. 46), 47, table 3–2(p. 48), tables B–1 to B–3(pp. 146–47); in self-image, 117; and sexual self, table 5–1(p. 62), table B–7(p. 151); and social self, table 4–1(p. 53), table 4–2(p. 55), table B–4 to B–6(pp. 148–50)

sex roles, 17, 97–98

sexual attitudes: of delinquent adolescents, 64; and normal adolescents, table B–7(p. 151); of physically ill adolescents, 116; and self-image, 106–7; and sex-related differences, 98; and the sexual self, 39

Sexual Attitudes scale, 61, 116, 140; and test results for all test groups, table E–7(p. 167); and test results for normal adolescents, table B–7(p. 151)

sexual conservatism, 106–7, 116

sexual drives, 4

sexual energy, and self-representation, 21

sexual impulses, of adults, 122

sexuality, 24, 93–94; and OSIQ results, 87, 88; and psychoanalytic theory of adolescence, 86; and sex-related differences, 62

sexual revolution, 107

sexual self, 61–64; and deviant adolescents, 63–64; test results for all test

groups, table E–7(p. 167); test results for normal adolescents, table B–7(p. 151); test scales for, 39

shame: of delinquent and disturbed adolescents, 78, 110; girls' feelings of, 95

Shaw, C. R., 111

single-parent households, 105

situational anxiety, 92–93, 117

situation-dependent self, 16

Sklansky, M. D., 4, 122

Smith, M. B., 15

social categories, and language, 19

social opportunities: and sex-related differences in self-image, 98–100

social recognition, 21

social relationships: and normal adolescents, 54; psychologically disturbed adolescents and difficulty with, 59; and sex-related differences, 95–101 passim; and the social self, 39

Social Relationships scale, 52, 140; and test results for all test groups, table E–4(p. 164); test results for normal adolescents, table B–4(p. 148)

Social Sciences Computer Program, and analyses of variance, 156

social self, 52–70; of deviant adolescent, 58–59; test results for all test groups, tables E–4 to E–6(pp. 164–66); test results for normal adolescents, tables B–4 to B–6(pp. 148–50); test scales for, 39

social sensitivity, and sex-related differences, 95

social systems, 52

social values, and sex-related differences, 55–56, table 4–2(p. 55)

social vulnerability and physically ill adolescents, 77

socioeconomic background, of test sample, 34

solitude and delinquent adolescents, 58

splitting off, 20

Srole, L., 94, 106

stability in family, 65

stability of personality, 119–21

standard deviation: derivation of, 38; on OSIQ, table C–1(p. 157)

standard scores, 32, table D–1(p. 158)

stress-inducing nature of adolescence, 94

study of self, 26–29